THE SCHOOL ZONE

THE SCHOOL ZONE

JOHN DUCKWORTH

VICTOR BOOKS
A DIVISION OF SCRIPTURE PRESS PUBLICATIONS INC.
USA CANADA ENGLAND

More Young Teen Feedback Electives

Nobody Like Me by Stan Campbell
For Real People Only by Sandy Larsen
What's Your Problem? by Karen Dockrey
Family Survival Guide by Karen Dockrey
Friends—Who Needs Them? by Lin Johnson

Third printing, 1989

Library of Congress Catalog Card Number: 86-60866
ISBN: 0-89693-198-6

CONTENTS

THE SCHOOL ZONE is designed to help your young teens learn to live out their faith at school and cope with concerns about problems such as peer pressure, competition, relationships, and authority in a school setting. As part of the Young Teen Feedback Elective series, this book presents creative Bible studies that will keep your young teens interested and challenge them to spiritual growth.

HOW TO USE YOUNG TEEN FEEDBACK ELECTIVES

You'll discover that these studies are especially geared toward young teens—a group in the midst of change. As they struggle to make the transition from children to adults, young teens sometimes show extremes of behavior—energetic one minute, withdrawn the next. These fast-paced studies offer a variety of teaching methods to appeal to sometimes hard-to-interest group members. Yet each creative session is firmly founded on the Word of God.

Each lesson focuses on one or more Bible truths that can be applied directly to young teens' lives. Make sure you have enough Bibles so that students who forget theirs can borrow them. Try to have some modern-speech translations on hand for easy comprehension.

If you're unfamiliar with Young Teen Feedback Electives, take a few minutes to study this overview of your elective study.

Flexible Format

Notice that you can study the topic of this book over a 12-week quarter. In addition, each subtopic is complete in itself, so you can also study part of this elective for four weeks, returning to the other studies at a later time. This format gives you flexibility to suit your program to the particular needs of your young people. It also lets you tailor the study to your schedule.

Introductory Page

Each session has an easy-to-use summary of the lesson on the first page to help you see the lesson at a glance.

- *Key Concept* clearly states the lesson's theme.
- *Meeting the Need* outlines general concerns and questions young teens have on the session's subject. By understanding their concerns, you can better help teens apply the lesson.
- *Session Goals* includes the objectives of the lesson in measurable terms. Each goal helps communicate the Key Concept and should be achieved by group members by the end of the session.
- *Special Preparation* gives you a checklist of what you'll need to lead the session.

Building the Body

The first minutes of each session are devoted to relationship building. These exercises, activities, and optional "warm-ups" will help your group get to know one another and you—a key to an open group where good communication can take place. These activities also provide a transition time which takes young teens away from outside concerns and points them toward the group study.

Launching the Lesson
This section offers focus discussions and activities that zero in on needs and interests that will be covered by the Bible study later in the lesson.

Exploring the Word
This part of the study contains creative ways to communicate Bible truths and concepts. It not only helps *you* share God's Word, but it also allows young teens to discover God's Word for themselves.

Applying the Truth
This application section summarizes Bible truths and concepts. It helps young teens relate Christian faith and values to their everyday lives, answering the question, "What does this mean to me?"

Workout Sheets
These activity sheets encourage young teens to discover concepts, facts, and ideas in a variety of ways. The sheets are meant to be reproduced. Just tear out the master copy and make as many duplicates as you need. You may want to provide folders for group members to collect and save their Workout Sheets.

Student Books
Student books are available to help bring home Bible truths to young teens in your group. These lively books are written by men and women who know how to communicate to your young people. They can be used many different ways:

■ Have group members read the chapter *after* each session so material covered in class will be reinforced and "come alive" at home.

■ Have group members read a chapter *before* each session to stimulate their thinking on the subject and get them ready for in-class discussions.

■ Use portions of the books *during* the group study. For instance, incorporate a case study from the book into a group discussion.

You can complete this elective study without using the student books, but we recommend them as an excellent tool to give students their own version of the material you study together. It's something permanent that they can refer to long after the group study has ended.

These books are entertaining, informative, and fun to use. Their small size makes them portable; they fit easily into pockets or purses. Look for them at your local Christian bookstore, and add them to this elective study.

Before Each Lesson
Pray for your young teens as they work through this study. Ask the Lord to help you create an open atmosphere in your group, so that teens will feel free to share with each other and you.

After Each Lesson
Evaluate each session as you ask yourself the following questions: Did each student achieve the lesson goals? Why or why not? Did you have the right amount of time to complete the lesson? How many group members actively took part in the session? Are interpersonal relationships being nurtured in the group? How well did you prepare the lesson? How might you change your presentation next time?

The School Zone Blues

PART ONE

What do your young teens think about school? They *don't* think first—they *feel.* Those Sunday-night groans at the swift approach of Monday morning, those chills at the mention of an essay test, those pangs of loneliness in the middle of a crowded hallway—all testify to the sometimes overwhelming emotions that whirl like windstorms in The School Zone.

That's why your journey through this dimension begins with a look at school-related stress, fear, loneliness, and anger. You'll give your students a chance to say and show how they feel about the agonies and ecstasies of their "real" world, school. Then you'll help them discover how the life and teachings of Christ can make that world a less tiring, less threatening, less lonely, less irritating place. That's important because the law says they have to stay there whether they like it or not. You can help them survive, maybe even thrive, as you teach them the benefits of taking Jesus into a place they may think He's never been—The School Zone.

These sessions may be used independently, as a four-week unit, or as part of the quarterly study. Feel free to adapt the plans to fit your group; listen as they discuss their school-related feelings so that you'll know which points to emphasize. If you're using the correlated student book, also entitled *The School Zone,* assign each upcoming week's chapter for students to read. If you haven't already done so, try to visit each of the schools represented in your group to get a clearer picture of what your young teens face five days a week. They'll be glad you did—and so will you.

THE SCHOOL ZONE BLUES

SESSION 1

THE HEAT IS ON

KEY CONCEPT

The hard work of school causes stress, but it doesn't have to overwhelm us if we follow Jesus' example of dealing with pressure.

MEETING THE NEED

This session will respond to student questions and comments like these:

- "English class is killing me."
- "Every Sunday night I get this pain in my stomach because I know I have to go to school the next day."
- "Junior high is ten times harder than grade school."

SESSION GOALS

You'll help each group member

1. explore his or her feelings about school,
2. identify sources of school stress,
3. discover that setting priorities, keeping in touch with God, and allowing rest times can help reduce that "pressured" feeling.

SPECIAL PREPARATION

_____ If you plan to use the "Building the Body" activity called "Priority Pile-up" and must do it indoors, you'll need a roll of adhesive tape to mark off your playing area.

_____ If you do "Final Exam," remember to bring pencils and paper, plus a radio or other noisemaking device. If you want to award prizes, bring enough for the whole group.

BUILDING THE BODY

Try one or both of the following activities to get your students involved and thinking about stress.

PRIORITY PILE-UP

This game is ideal for an outdoor meeting, but will work indoors if you mark off a four-foot-square (or larger, depending on the size of your group) playing area with adhesive tape. Allow plenty of room around the square. Start by packing the square with as many standing students as you can. Tell them that the object of the game is to get and keep as many people as possible in the playing area—but that they must also obey the commands you will call out. Everyone starts the game with 10 points. If even one person falls or is pushed outside the square while an order is being followed, everyone loses a point. Then call out the following orders, allowing time after each one for the players to comply:

1. Touch your toes.
2. Stretch out your arms as far as you can.
3. Bend your arms and flap them chicken-style.
4. Turn all the way around.
5. Run in place.
6. Arrange yourselves in alphabetical order (by last names).
7. Close your eyes and turn around.
8. Stand on one leg.
9. Do your impression of the Statue of Liberty.
10. Touch the floor with both hands.

When all the orders have been followed, award prizes according to the number of points students have left (a penny or piece of candy per point, for instance, depending on the size of your group and budget). Then explain that you've just demonstrated how hard it is to follow two orders ("Stay in the square" and "Touch the floor," for example) when they conflict. To survive, you've got to decide which is more important to you—or to put it another way, you've got to set your priorities.

FINAL EXAM

Split your group into pairs. One person in each pair is to take the "exam" while the other watches him to guard against cheating. Pass out paper and pencil to each exam-taker. The assignment: Write down the alphabet—backward. Begin with Z, and end with A. Monitors must watch to make sure their partners don't start at the bottom of the paper with A and work back to Z; that would be too easy. When all is ready, say, "Go!" and switch on a radio or other noisemaker to add to the examinees' stress. The first to complete the backward alphabet wins.

After the contest, ask students why their assignment was harder than just writing the alphabet (they had to write it backward, they were being watched, and the noise made it harder to concentrate). Observe that we face these kinds of stress at school; the work is harder than in previous grades, teachers and parents are watching us, and all sorts of other pressures can make it hard to concentrate.

LAUNCHING THE LESSON

Explain that in the coming weeks you're going to talk about "real life"—the things that happen in your students' lives between 8 A.M. and 3 P.M., five days a week. Say something like this: **Do you know how much time you spend at school? If you go to school from 8 A.M. to 3 P.M. five days a week, that's 35 hours a week. If you go 35 weeks a year, that's 1,225 hours a year. If you go for 12 years, that's 14,700 hours! If you were paid minimum wage for those hours, you'd make about $50,000. Maybe that wouldn't be so crazy, because going to school can be a pretty tough job. It can put a lot of pressure on you in a lot of ways, and that's what we're going to talk about today.**

WORKOUT SHEET

Distribute Workout Sheet #1, "School Stress Maze." As your students complete the sheet, assure them that everybody feels "pressured" at school at least part of the time; they should feel free to mark their stress levels as high or as low as they like. If they have trouble grasping the idea of stress, or relating it to their school lives, draw from examples like these:

1. Lunchroom: You don't have a best friend to sit with, so you feel out of place.
2. Math class: You get a "drowning" feeling here because you can't quite figure out problems like, "X over 12 equals 2, so what does X equal?"
3. Locker room: You almost hate to go in here after P.E. class because the same person always snaps you with a wet towel.
4. Science class: This teacher seems to have decided that you're a troublemaker, so he always calls on you when you don't have the answer.
5. History class: You get so much homework from this class that you feel like you'll never get it all done.

When your students have completed the Stress Maze, discuss their answers in as much detail as they're willing to reveal. Ask more reticent students where they feel the *least* pressure, which may give a clue as to which stressful situations they want to avoid. If you have time, add up the scores for various areas to see where your students' school "pressure points" are located. Keep these in mind during the rest of the sessions, concentrating on these areas when appropriate.

School pressures can affect our bodies as well as our minds. You already know that feeling you get in the pit of your stomach when the teacher calls for homework and you haven't got it, or you suddenly remember there's going to be a test and it's going to count 50 percent of your grade. If you feel too pressured for too long, it can actually make you sick. But you don't have to let school stress run your life. Jesus has a better idea.

EXPLORING THE WORD

SCRIPTURE SEARCH

Divide the group into two Scripture search teams: the "Work Crew" and the "Rescue Squad." Assign the Work Crew to read as many of the following passages as they can: Matthew 4:23-25; 12:9-12; 14:9-14; Mark 1:45–2:4; 3:20-21; and John 21:25. Assign the Rescue Squad to look at Matthew 14:22-23; Mark 1:35-38; 6:31-32; and 8:11-13.

Hurry both groups along in their reading, echoing Jesus' always-on-the-go work schedule as contained in these passages. When the teams are done (or it's time to move on), bring them back together to report on Christ's stressful schedule and His methods of dealing with stress.

Ask the Work Crew the following questions, referring them to the correct passages if necessary: **What kinds of work did Jesus do when He was on earth, according to these verses?** He traveled, taught in the synagogues, preached, and healed people (Matthew 4:23-25). **Did He always get weekends off?** No, He got in trouble with the Pharisees for healing a man on the Sabbath (Matthew 12:9-12). **Did He get to take time off when His friend John the Baptist was killed?** He tried to, but the crowds kept following Him, and He decided to heal their sick (Matthew 14:9-14). **How easy was it for Him to get away from all the people and pressures?** Not very. Eventually, He couldn't enter a town without crowds coming to meet Him, and a house He preached in was so crowded that a sick man had to be let down through the roof to get to Him (Mark 1:45–2:4). **Did everybody feel sorry for Him having to work so hard?** No. His family thought He was crazy to do it (Mark 3:20-21). **How does the last verse in John's Gospel let us know that Jesus was incredibly busy?** John writes that if everything Jesus did were to be written down, the whole world couldn't contain the records (John 21:25).

Then ask the Rescue Squad: **According to the verses you read, whom did Jesus talk to about the pressures He was facing?** He talked to His Father, God, in prayer (Matthew 14:22-23; Mark 1:35). Other verses show that He did this regularly, going off by Himself for quite a while to do it. **Did He work constantly without a rest?** No. He told His disciples to come away with Him to a quiet place to rest (Mark 6:31-32). **How do we know that Jesus had certain priorities—that He didn't try to do everything everybody wanted Him to do?** When Simon said everyone was looking for Jesus, wanting to be healed, Jesus went instead to other villages in order to preach; He said that was why He had come (Mark 1:36-38). When the Pharisees asked Him to do a miracle to show He was from God, He refused and left. He didn't come to earth to show off (Mark 8:11-13).

After using the preceding summary to fill gaps in your teams' reports, explain how Jesus' example and teachings can help us deal with pressures at school: **In His three years of ministry, Jesus did far more work than any of us could do during seventh, eighth, and ninth grades—maybe even in our whole lives. Yet He didn't get "stressed out." Why? Because He was always telling God about the pressures He faced. He talked to God honestly and regularly, asking Him for help. Jesus also knew what His priorities were—what He wanted to accomplish. Sometimes He had to turn down a perfectly good thing (like healing**

people) in order to do something more important.

Are we more powerful than Jesus? Of course not. We need to stay in touch with God too, telling Him what's going on with us and asking for His help. If the only time we pray is when we say grace before a meal, then we're only talking to God for about seven minutes a week—at the most. That's not much when you remember that in that same week we go through about 35 hours worth of school pressures. And just like Jesus, we can't do everything; some things are more important than others. We can't always watch what's on TV *and* do our homework, or belong to every club we like. We have to decide what's most important and do those things first. And just like Jesus and His disciples, we need to rest sometimes.

Rest is something Jesus promises us if we've received Him as our Saviour. (Read Matthew 11:28-30.) **The rest Jesus promises isn't just taking a nap or a vacation; it's being able to tell our pressures to Him, to know that He cares and is strong enough to work things out for our good. It's a trade—our pressured feelings for His peace.** (Read John 14:27.) **It doesn't mean that we ignore our problems; it means we remember how much bigger God is than our school stresses are.** (Read Matthew 6:25-27, 34.)

APPLYING THE TRUTH

STUDENT BOOK OPTION

Have each student make a list of the activities that take up his free time after school and on weekends. Then, in a separate list, each person should list his top 5–10 priorities (daily devotions, homework, household chores, etc.). Comparing the two lists, each person should make a sample schedule of one school night, designating time spent on priority activities and free time left over. Your young teens may need individual help with this and may wish to make more detailed schedules later.

WORKOUT SHEET

Distribute Workout Sheet #2, "Stressbusters!" Give students plenty of time to think about and record their answers. Remind them of the pressure points they located on their Stress Maps; they may use one of these, but encourage them to be specific about a pressure they're likely to face during the coming week. After the sheets are completed, ask volunteers to share answers with the rest of the group. You may want to make the following points as you guide the discussion:

- **We may think at first that the source of stress has to go away before our pressured feelings can decrease. But just as Jesus coped with stress that didn't go away, we can learn to change our reactions to pressures. We'll always have stress in our lives, so there's no point in waiting for "someday" when everything will be perfect and we can relax.**

- **It's easy to pray, "Lord, help me with this problem," and sit back, waiting for God to rush in like the A-Team and solve everything for us. But He wants to hear more from us than that. He may even want us to learn something through the stress, so we need to ask Him whether we're part of the problem. We should start by telling Him honestly how we feel, remembering that He knows all about pressure because He created us—and because His Son went through more stress than most people ever will.**

- **After we've talked to God, talking with another person about our pressures can be a good stressbuster. Jesus had 12 disciples to talk to, though they didn't always understand Him. "Who you gonna call" when you've got a problem?** (Note students' answers. If they don't mention any church or youth group leaders, you may want to find out whether some bridge-building needs to be done.)

- **It may be hard for us to imagine what Jesus would do if He were having trouble in Spanish class or couldn't seem to get His homework in on time. But based on the verses we looked at today, it's safe to say that He would most likely (1) talk with His Heavenly Father about it, (2) decide whether He needed to give up something else in order to solve the problem, and (3) believe that God would help with a solution. He would feel peaceful instead of pressured because He would know His Father cares about everything—including school.**

If time and the nature of your group allow, close the session with prayer for the specific stressful situations your students have mentioned. Offer your own concern and ready ear too, for future reference.

THE SCHOOL ZONE BLUES

SESSION 2

THE PANIC BUTTON

KEY CONCEPT

God understands our school-related fears and wants us to trust Him instead of being afraid.

MEETING THE NEED

You'll respond in this session to student questions and comments like these:

- "What if I flunk one of my classes?"
- "There's so much violence in my school that I'm afraid to walk down the hall sometimes."
- "I'm scared of having to get up and talk in class."

SESSION GOALS

You'll help each group member

1. realize that everyone is afraid of something,
2. recognize his or her school-related fears,
3. see that trusting God is better than hitting the panic button.

SPECIAL PREPARATION

_____ You may want to bring a stopwatch or other impressive timepiece for the "Building the Body" activity called "Stoneface," but any watch with a second hand or function will do.

BUILDING THE BODY

The following not-too-scary activities will help your group members approach the subject of fear—and have fun at the same time. Use one or both, depending on the time you have available.

STONEFACE

Place two chairs in front of the group, face to face. Have two volunteers sit in the chairs; one person is to try to make the other smile in 30 seconds or less without touching him or her. The rest of the group is to remain as quiet as possible, but the "comedian" can tell jokes, make faces, get up and run around, etc., in an attempt to make the "stoneface" smile. If the stoneface doesn't crack a smile within 30 seconds, he or she wins and gets to play the comedian for the next stoneface. If the comedian succeeds, he plays stoneface for a new comedian. If "cracking up" stonefaces gets too easy after a few rounds, reduce the time limit to 15 seconds. When you're done, vote on the funniest comedian and stoniest stoneface. Use the game as an illustration when the lesson begins, explaining that just as the stonefaces didn't want to crack a smile, we often try to hide our emotions—especially when that emotion is fear.

LEAST FAVORITE THINGS

Going around the circle (or up and down the rows, depending on your seating arrangement), present each student with one of the following choices. If he or she *had* to do one of these two scary things, which would he or she choose, and why? If others would choose differently, allow them to briefly vocalize their reasons too.

1. Hold a nonpoisonous, live snake—or eat a plateful of liver and onions.
2. Make a speech in a school assembly—or go to the dentist to get a tooth filled.
3. Climb onto the roof of your house—or let a daddy longlegs spider crawl across the back of your hand.
4. Sing a solo in the church service—or sing a solo in your Sunday School class.
5. Spend 10 minutes in a room with a wasp buzzing around you—or eat a chocolate-covered ant.
6. Sell magazine subscriptions to strangers door-to-door—or over the phone.
7. Roller skate—or ice skate.
8. Walk through a cemetery in the middle of the night—or ask someone for a date for the first time.
9. Visit someone in the hospital—or take a test in your hardest class.
10. Fly in a plane—or present a class petition to the President of the United States.

Your students may suggest that they're not *afraid* of some things, just *disgusted* by them (eating liver, for instance). But point out that psychologists say we're disgusted by things when we're afraid of how they'd feel in our mouths or on our bodies. So disgust is probably based on fear. Use your students' choices to show that even though we may think we're not afraid of anything, some things scare us enough that we want to avoid them. And what seems easy to one person may cause fear for another.

LAUNCHING THE LESSON

DISCUSSION

Ask your students whether they ever have nightmares. If they say yes, ask one or two students to describe a couple of those bad dreams. If no one will admit having nightmares, tell the group about one of your own, emphasizing the fear you felt. Then ask whether anyone in the group ever has nightmares about *school*. Give volunteers a chance to answer. Then explain: **Many people occasionally have bad dreams involving school. Some adults even have these nightmares long after graduation. Here are a few school situations some people dream about:**

- **Getting lost. The hallways are suddenly unfamiliar and complicated, like a maze. The school building seems huge, and you can't find any of your classes—especially the one you're supposed to be in next.**

- **Forgetting a class. It's the middle of the semester, and all at once you remember that you signed up for a class at the start of the year—but haven't attended it more than once or twice. There's no way you could possibly catch up now; you're bound to flunk.**

- **Forgetting your locker combination. This happens in real life, of course, but it may happen more often in dreamland. Just as in real life, it happens right when you absolutely have to get into your locker to get a book or your gym clothes.**

- **Forgetting what you were going to say. You're up in front of a bunch of people—giving a speech or report or acting in a play—and suddenly your mind goes blank. You feel like melting into a little blob on the floor.**

Have you ever had any dreams like that? (Allow students to answer; if possible, list on a chalkboard or easel the school nightmares mentioned above, along with those described by students.) **Why do you think people have these nightmares?** (Usually because they're afraid these things might actually happen to them.) **Our fears are often revealed in our bad dreams. For example, a person who dreams about getting lost at school may be afraid that school is getting too big or complicated for him. What other fears might lie behind the other nightmares we've mentioned?** (Some possible answers: A person who dreams about forgetting a class or locker combination may fear being unprepared for a test; a nightmare about forgetting a speech may indicate fear of making a fool of oneself; dreaming about a threatening person may reveal fear of a bully, a gang, or even a teacher.)

Having nightmares like these doesn't mean you're crazy. Even though school can seem like a pretty safe—even boring—place, it

can be a pretty scary place at other times. Say you're new at school; what might be scary about that? (Not knowing where things are, whether kids will like you, whether classes will be hard or easy, or whether your teachers will be crabby or easy to get along with.) **What else about school is scary sometimes?** (Not knowing whether you'll pass a test or a class, whether you'll make the cheerleading squad, whether that older and bigger kid will pound you into the ground like he said he would, whether you'll be able to play your trumpet solo in the band concert, or whether you'll break your neck doing gymnastics in P.E. class.)

Not knowing—that's our biggest fear. We wonder what's going to happen to us; we ask ourselves, "What if. . . ?" "What if I miss the bus? What if they laugh at me when I say I'm a Christian? What if I don't make this shot during the basketball game?" There's only one Person who can answer all those "What if?" questions, and that's God. So let's look at His Word to find out how He can help us when our fears make us feel like hitting the panic button.

EXPLORING THE WORD

WORKOUT SHEET

Distribute Workout Sheet #3, "Can You Read My Mind?" Since this exercise requires looking up verses *and* using imagination, allow students plenty of time. If they need an example to get them started, have a student read Matthew 14:25-27 aloud. Then say something like this: **It was very dark out on the lake—past the middle of the night. All of a sudden the disciples looked into the distance and saw a dim figure that seemed to float on top of the water. No, it was *walking* on top of the water! It had to be a ghost! The disciples were panicking. What would *you* have thought if you'd been in their sandals?** (Wait for an answer. The disciples might have thought, "Lemme outta here!" or "Where's Jesus now that we need Him?" or "What's that? A ghost! Help! I think I'm having a heart attack! We're all gonna die!" Any logical answer will do.) After students have completed their sheets, ask them to tell what happened in the passages and share the contents of their thought balloons. If necessary, summarize the disciples' panicked reactions in the three remaining passages (summaries in parentheses).

- **Matthew 14:28-31** (Peter must have thought walking on water was a great new sport—or he wanted to make sure the "ghost" was really Jesus. He climbed over the side of the boat, stepped onto the water, and actually walked a few steps before he remembered what he was doing. He may have thought something like, "Hey! What am I doing? Look at those waves! I can't walk on a lake! What if Jesus can't hold me up?" And he sank.)

- **Mark 4:35-40** (This time Jesus was in the boat, not on the water. A big storm came up. Jesus just kept sleeping on a pillow in the back of the boat. Again the disciples panicked, no doubt thinking something like, "We're going to drown! Why doesn't Jesus wake up? If the boat goes under, He can always *walk* to shore—but what's going to happen to *us*?")

- **Matthew 17:1-8** (Jesus took three of the disciples up on a mountain. All of a sudden He started to glow. It was like a "special effect," only real. That was scary enough, but then two of the most famous men in Israel's history appeared. They'd been dead for hundreds of years, but there they were, talking to Jesus! The disciples may have thought, "What's going on? Is Jesus going to explode? Should we run? Kneel down?" Peter was so scared he started babbling about building three little shelters for Jesus, Moses, and Elijah to stand in. Great idea, huh?)

DISCUSSION

The disciples were a lot like us. They had the "what ifs." They were afraid of not knowing. But deeper than that, all the way at the bottom of their fears, was something else. It's in the answer to the last question on your sheet. What was the *real* reason the disciples panicked? (They didn't have faith, didn't believe, didn't trust God enough to take care of them.) **That's what fear is all about—not trusting God enough. The disciples had already seen Jesus do fantastic miracles, but they still didn't trust Him to be able to take care of *everything.* They didn't realize yet who Jesus is. They kept asking each other, "Who *is* this?" How would you answer their question?** (He's God, the Son of God.)

The disciples finally figured that out, and it changed their lives. They saw that Jesus has all the power in the universe—and more—available to Him. After Jesus rose from the dead, they stopped being afraid of their own shadows and went out to tell the world about Him. They were so sure that Jesus had gone to prepare a place for them in heaven that they risked getting killed in order to spread the Good News. Most of them *were* killed—so that people like us would know about Jesus.

The Lord understands how hard it is for us to believe sometimes, but He's still asking us a question today. It's in Mark 4:40. What is it? ("Why are you so afraid? Do you still have no faith?")

APPLYING THE TRUTH

WORKOUT SHEET

Distribute Workout Sheet #4, "What If. . . ?" Encourage your young teens to keep their worst-case scenarios realistic. For example, a bad report card might lead to being grounded or having to repeat a class—but would probably not *really* mean "my folks would kill me." When students have completed their sheets, discuss their answers. Some possible worst cases: (1) The teacher might get mad at you for not having your book or for being late, or you could be sent to the principal's office for being in the hall after the bell rings. (2) Your parents could punish you or you might not be able to get into some college programs. (3) You might embarrass yourself at tryouts and/or not get a part in the play. (4) The principal might expel you or tell you some bad news about an accident involving a family member. (5) You might forget what you were going to say, your voice might crack, your zipper might be undone, and the other kids might laugh at you. (6) The other student might beat you up—maybe injuring you seriously or even killing you.

DISCUSSION

Ask: **Which of these "worst things" would be too hard for God to help you through?** (If someone suggests such a case, hear him or her out without being judgmental. Express the hope that as you learn more about God together, you'll find reasons to trust Him with even the hardest situations. More likely, your students will know the "right" answer is that nothing is too hard for God—making them reluctant to admit that it can be hard to trust Him. If so, point out that even though we "know" God is to be trusted, we sometimes find it tough to stop being scared. If you are using the student book, ask: **What "monsters" like the ones in the haunted house has God helped you get past?** (Answers will vary.) Read Jeremiah 29:11 and ask: **How does knowing that God has plans for you encourage you?** (He can be trusted with the future.)

Read the following passages aloud, asking students to list the reasons Jesus gives for not being afraid:

- **Matthew 10:19-20** (God can give us the words when we don't know what to say.)
- **Matthew 10:28-31** (Even a person who kills the body can't kill the soul; God protects the "real us"; God knows all about us all the time, right down to the hairs on our heads, so we can trust Him to know about our scary situations; God considers us worth taking care of.)
- **John 14:1-4** (Jesus is preparing a great future in heaven for those who have received Him, and He has told us how to get there.)
- **John 16:33** (Jesus has overcome the world, which means He is more powerful than any enemy.)

Encourage your students to bring Jesus' "overcoming" power with them to school by remembering that last verse. If time allows, help them to memorize it. Then close in prayer, asking the Lord to remind your students this week why they can trust Him instead of hitting the panic button.

THE SCHOOL ZONE BLUES

SESSION 3

ALL BY YOURSELF?

KEY CONCEPT

We don't have to feel alone at school if we stay close to Jesus Christ.

MEETING THE NEED

This session will help students deal with concerns like these:

- "Nobody at school likes me."
- "Our school is so big that I just feel like a number."
- "I always feel like an outsider."

SESSION GOALS

You'll help each group member

1. realize that loneliness is not necessarily caused by "weirdness,"
2. understand that Jesus went through extreme loneliness so that we wouldn't have to,
3. consider his or her closeness to Jesus at school.

SPECIAL PREPARATION

_____ If you plan to use the "Building the Body" activity called "Listen to the Lonely," contact a few group members during the week. Ask them to check their music collections for songs about loneliness. Borrow a few of these records and tapes, screen them, and bring them to the meeting along with appropriate playback equipment. Recent songs which will be familiar to students are preferred, though "oldies" and many country-western songs are about loneliness too.

_____ If you decide to play "Backwardball" as an opener, bring a foam rubber ball and hoop (available in toy stores), beanbag and fruit basket, or other such combination.

_____ Be sure to make copies of the skit, "I'm So Lonely," included in "Launching the Lesson." Give the copies to three students before the session, explaining their roles. Practice the skit once or twice if necessary.

BUILDING THE BODY

Try either or both of these activities; one creates a mood, while the other will provide you with an analogy later in the lesson.

LISTEN TO THE LONELY

Obtain a few loneliness-related popular songs as noted under "Special Preparation." Have these or other songs playing as students arrive. When the group is assembled, explain that you've gathered some songs you'd like them to listen to; then play a couple that express the poignant feeling of being "all alone." Follow the music with a discussion of how the songwriters and musicians have described loneliness. What caused the lonely feelings in the songs? Did listening to the songs create lonely feelings in your students? Did the songs offer solutions to loneliness? When a person feels lonely, does it help or hurt to listen to these songs? The point is not to produce "right" answers to the questions, but to get your young teens thinking about the emotions the songs portray.

BACKWARDBALL

See who can make the most consecutive baskets, using a foam rubber ball and hoop, beanbag and fruit basket, or similar equipment. Line your students up at the "foul line" of your choosing—but *backward*. They must make their shots with their backs to the goal. When this proves to be a frustrating experience, point out that it's hard to see things as they are when we're facing the wrong direction. Use this experience later to illustrate how we can't feel Christ's constant presence with us at school if we turn our backs on Him.

LAUNCHING THE LESSON

A PLAY

While you set up three chairs in front of the group, announce that you're all about to see a play. Have the three students to whom you've given copies of the following lines go into the hall or elsewhere to await their entrances. Say: **This play takes place at (name of a junior high school represented in your group). It's about the thoughts of three students who happen to sit on the same bench under the same tree on the same afternoon—but don't know each other.**

(*The first student enters, looking gloomy, and sits in one of the chairs with his chin resting on his hand. He sighs, then speaks sadly as if thinking aloud.)* I'm so lonely in this school. The other kids have all the friends they need, but nobody likes me. Everybody else is in some clique, but not me. I'm probably the only Christian in the whole school. There must be something wrong with me to make me feel so alone. Nobody else feels lonely. *(The second student enters, acting just like the first, sits down, and says exactly the same things the first student said. Neither student pays attention to the other. After the second student finishes, the third student enters as the other two did, sits next to them, and says exactly the same things in the same way. There is a pause, and the three students sigh. They look at each other, then go back to their gloomy poses, and say sadly in unison:)* If only I could be happy like everybody else. *(They sigh once more, then exit.)*

DISCUSSION

After leading a round of applause for your actors, ask: **What can we learn about loneliness from these three people?** (We all feel lonely sometimes, but we think we're the only ones who feel that way.) **What are some of the reasons why a person might feel lonely at school?** (It's probably best to keep the questions in the third person at this point, since those who feel painfully lonely probably won't want to "give themselves away"—and those who don't feel lonely at the moment won't want others to think they don't have any friends. Aid the discussion as needed by mentioning the following reasons for loneliness at school.)

- **Being new. If you don't know anybody, it's no wonder you feel lonely. If you have had to move a lot, you know how alone you feel on that first day in a new school.**

- **Feeling rejected or shut out. If your school is divided into cliques and you're not in any of them, you're probably going to feel alone. If you find it hard to talk to kids you don't know, you may keep to yourself for fear of being rejected. If you tried to make friends and it didn't seem to work out, you may be afraid to try again.**

- **Feeling like an ant in a very big anthill. If your school is large, it may seem like nobody knows you or cares to. You may feel like a number, or a little part in a machine.**

- **Missing somebody. Maybe you used to have a good friend who moved away, or you lost a member of your family and feel lonely in general.**

- **Feeling different from everybody else. Maybe you think you're the only Christian in your school, or the only guy who doesn't like football, or the only girl who doesn't understand how to look like the models in *Seventeen* magazine. Maybe you even think you're the only one who's ever lonely, like the people in the skit, and that being lonely means you're weird. That only makes you feel lonelier.**

Having that "all by yourself" feeling doesn't mean you're weird. There were plenty of times when Jesus felt that way. We're going to look at some of those times, and figure out why the Bible says we don't have to feel alone anymore.

EXPLORING THE WORD

WORKOUT SHEET

Distribute Workout Sheet #5, "The Loneliest Man in the World." It may take a while for your students to read all the verses involved; let them work in groups to save time.

When the exercise is completed, discuss the answers. All the people listed on the sheet turned away from Christ at some time, so all should be crossed out. Ask whether students know *why* Jesus was so rejected. As needed, use the following summary to explain.

People from His hometown rejected Jesus because they thought prophets could only come from *other* towns. Members of His family—probably His brothers—denied Him until He rose from the dead because they thought prophets could only come from other *families*. Fellow synagogue members wanted to throw Jesus over a cliff because He compared them to Old Testament Israelites who rejected the prophets.

The disciples promised never to desert Jesus, but every single one did. They were afraid of being arrested for following Him. The religious leaders wanted to get rid of Jesus because He said they were hypocrites, and He claimed to be the Son of God.

The crowds called for Jesus' execution because they'd been egged on by the religious leaders; Pilate turned his back on Jesus to satisfy the crowds. The passersby, soldiers, and men on the other crosses rejected Jesus because they figured He couldn't possibly be the Messiah as He'd claimed. They thought God's Son would never let Himself be slapped around, spat on, tortured, and executed.

And then there was God. Why would God turn away? Jesus had served His Heavenly Father perfectly all His life, but in the last minutes before He died Jesus cried out, "My God, My God, why have You forsaken Me?" (Mark 15:34) **God had to turn away from Jesus at the end because of *us*. Jesus had taken on the sins of the whole world, including ours, so that His death could pay for them. God had to turn away because He hates sin—and when He looked at Jesus on that cross, He saw the whole world's sin concentrated in one Man.**

Nobody else in history has ever been so alone. A few of the people who loved Him, including His mother, were at the foot of the cross when He died, but they couldn't help Him. Everyone else had rejected Him. Do you know anybody at school who's *that* alone? (Probably not.)

Let's say that tomorrow morning everybody at school turns his back on you. No student, teacher, or administrator will have anything to do with you. People you thought were friends suddenly say they never even met you. Your teachers give you an F on every paper even if you deserve an A. The principal calls you into his office, falsely claims that you committed some crime, and hands you over to the police. They throw you in jail, beat you up, and some crooked judge gives

you the death penalty. Nobody protests. Nobody steps forward to say you're innocent. Within 24 hours the prison guards grab you and take you to be executed. On a scale of one to ten, how lonely would you feel? (Ten or eleven, most likely.) **But you wouldn't be as alone as Jesus was. Do you know why?** (Because God wouldn't turn His back on you.)

Jesus became the loneliest Man in the world so that we would never have to be alone again. (Read, or have a student read, John 14:15-21.) **Who is this Counselor, this Spirit of Truth?** (The Holy Spirit.) **Where does Jesus say the Holy Spirit will be?** (In us—those who receive Christ.) **Where will Jesus Himself be?** (In those who love and obey Him.)

Jesus made a promise to those who follow Him. It's in the very last sentence of the Gospel of Matthew. (Have a student read Matthew 28:20.) **Oh, wait a minute, you must have read that wrong. That's supposed to be, "I will always be with you, except at school." Would you read it again, exactly the way it's written?** (Wait for student to read it again.) **No, no, that's not right. You must have the Weirdo Version. Let's have somebody else read it.** (Choose another to read it.) **Now, wait a minute. Doesn't it say, "Except when you feel lonely"? How about, "Except when you forget I'm there"?** (Wait for negative response.) **Hmm. Well, then, what about those three lonely Christians on the bench in the skit we saw earlier? Does that verse say, "Except when you're sitting on a bench"?** (Wait for a no.) **Well, you guys may have discovered something here. Maybe if Jesus says He and His Spirit are always going to be with us, He means *always*.**

STUDENT BOOK OPTION

Why did Kevin experience loneliness in The School Zone? (He changed schools eight times before finishing high school.) **How did he deal with his loneliness?** (Reminded himself that Jesus was with him; reached out to other lonely people.)

APPLYING THE TRUTH

WORKOUT SHEET

Pass around copies of Workout Sheet #6, "The Day Jesus Went to School." Encourage students to choose the words and phrases that truly reflect their feelings, not just the ones they think you want to hear. Toward that end, assure them that they won't have to share their answers unless they want to.

When the exercise is completed, allow students to comment on the story if they wish. If they say that none of the choices fits their feelings, ask them to describe their feelings in their own words. Then say something like this: **In a way, this was a made-up story. When we take Jesus to school, we don't see Him—and neither do other people. But in another way, this was a *true* story. If we've received Jesus as Saviour, we really are never alone because He's always with us. That means everywhere—in every class, at every lunch, on the bus, wherever we argue or have** a good time or do our homework or sit on a bench feeling like we're all alone.

How we treat our friend Jesus is up to us. We can ignore Him. We can pretend He's not there. We can turn our backs on Him. If we do that, it won't be any wonder if we feel alone. We will have *chosen* to feel that way.

Jesus knows what it's like to be *very* lonely. So He wants to help us with our loneliness—first by being with us Himself, then by giving us the courage to be with other people. Those three students in the skit all thought they were the only lonely ones, but of course they weren't. If they'd gotten to know each other a little, they might have found that out.

If you get that "all by yourself" feeling at school this week, remember what Jesus went through so that you wouldn't have to be alone. Stay close to Him. Then ask Him to lead you to another person who needs a friend. It may take a while, but Jesus won't let you down. After all, He knows how much it means to have a friend.

THE SCHOOL ZONE BLUES

SESSION 4

GOOD AND MAD

KEY CONCEPT

When problems and people at school make us angry, we should deal with anger as Jesus did—constructively, without hurting ourselves or others.

MEETING THE NEED

In this session you'll respond to student complaints like these:
- "I hate school!"
- "I've got this teacher who's so unfair."
- "Some of the kids at school are so stuck up it makes me sick."

SESSION GOALS

You'll help each group member
1. identify school-related irritations,
2. see that anger is a response that can be right or wrong,
3. consider biblical ways of handling anger and how they may be applied to school life.

SPECIAL PREPARATION

_____ If you use the "Unfair Game" as an opener, bring the items (including prizes) needed to play the game you choose.

_____ If you stage a "Blowup," get together with another adult during the week to plan your argument.

_____ "Weird Wally Walloon," the story used for "Launching the Lesson," deserves a practice read-through for maximum effect. If you decide to use a guest storyteller, give him or her a copy of that part of the lesson.

BUILDING THE BODY

Try one or both of the following activities to bring your group to a rollicking boil.

UNFAIR GAME

Bring the equipment for a game your young teens enjoy. After promising prizes to the winners, play the game as you usually would. But when the game is over and the winners are ready for their prizes, give the awards to the *losers*. The winners will no doubt protest your unfairness. Use this angry moment to explain that life is unfair sometimes—and not getting what we want or expect can make us pretty mad. (Once you've made your point, though, hand out prizes to the winners too. You don't want them to stay so angry with you that they fume all the way through the lesson.)

BLOWUP

If you're a bit of a ham, you and a friend can pull this one off. If not, obtain the services of two of your more extroverted students. The object is to stage a heated argument before the session begins. Stay within easy earshot of your group members, but don't obviously stand "front and center" to get their attention. The topic of your argument doesn't matter as long as it's logical; two adults could argue about who was supposed to prepare the lesson or who's going to pay for the fender-bender that just occurred in the parking lot. Two students could fight over money owed, a broken promise, clothing borrowed and ruined, or an imaginary romantic rivalry. Your exchange should last about half a minute, building in intensity and volume to a climactic, angry exit by one of the antagonists.

Let the group react for a few moments before you call the session to order. Then invite the departed "fighter" to come back as you explain that this wasn't a *real* argument. Ask students to identify the emotions they saw portrayed, and how it felt to watch the angry exchange. Point out that anger affects not only those who are angry, but also those who get caught in the crossfire. Tell the group that you're about to discuss *real* anger, not the staged kind, and thank your arguers for their performances.

LAUNCHING THE LESSON

WEIRD WALLY WALLOON

Begin by reading aloud the following story of "Weird Wally Walloon." Because it's a fairy tale of sorts, it should be delivered in an exaggerated, singsong, "Once upon a time" voice. To get into character, imagine that you're the host of a low-budget children's TV show. If you can't manage that, borrow a teacher who is a sharp storyteller from one of the children's classes in your Sunday School—preferably a sweet, grandmotherly lady who has a good sense of humor.

Say: **This morning, boys and girls, we have an extra special treat. We're going to hear a story—the story of Weird Wally Walloon. I know you'll want to listen closely because Wally goes to a school that's a lot like yours. And I'm sure you feel about your school exactly the same way that Wally feels about his. So here it is—the wonderful story of Weird Wally Walloon.**

Not far away, just a skip and a jump from the street where you live, you'll find Weird Wally Walloon. Weird Wally Walloon *loves* school. He loves it more than anything else in the world. In fact, he loves it so much that he jumps out of bed at 5:30 every morning just so he can write down in his diary all the wonderful things that happened to him at school the day before.

After breakfast, Wally rides the big orange bus to school. Oh, how Wally loves to ride that bus! He loves to sit in the back, where a thoughtful fellow student has left a large wad of chewing gum on the seat. The same friendly student likes to play a radio very loudly into Wally's ear and bash him repeatedly over the head with a lunch box. "Good morning," Wally tells his friend. "Thank you for allowing me to sit next to you."

At school, Wally opens his locker and finds that some other friendly students have filled it from top to bottom with shaving cream. "Oh, those wacky friends of mine," Wally says with a smile. "This is almost as much fun as the time they stole my wallet and set my pants on fire!" Finding his soggy books somewhere in the shaving cream, Wally heads for his classes.

Wally *loves* his classes. He loves his social studies class, where Miss Fangmeyer always assigns him at least 30 pounds of homework each day. He loves P.E. class, where Coach Crunchman makes him take 59 laps around the football field for not polishing his gym shoes. And he *especially* loves the school cafeteria, where his many friends threaten to pour their cartons of milk over his head unless he cleans up their trays for them.

Yes, Wally loves school—every minute of it. He can't understand why anyone would get mad about the wonderful things that happen to him every day. He hopes that he never, never *ever* has to graduate from junior high.

And *that's* why they call him Weird Wally Walloon. The end.

Thank your storyteller (if you didn't read the story yourself). Then say: **Wasn't that a great story? And so realistic! How many of you love everything that happens at school, just like Weird Wally Walloon?** (Wait for a show of hands, which you probably won't get.) **How would you feel if the things that happened to Wally happened to you?** (Angry, if not homicidal.) Explain that anger would be a normal response to these people and events; Wally is the one who's weird.

WORKOUT SHEET

Say: **Not too many people are as abused as the guy in our story. But**

plenty of things can happen at school that make you mad. Here's a sheet for writing down some of those things. Distribute Workout Sheet #7, "Your Temper Temperature." If your young people don't find their pet gripes on the list, tell them to write some in. When the sheets are finished, discuss the results to find out what's bugging your group members.

Say: **When something unfair happens to us, or when we want something to happen and it doesn't, we usually get angry. When we get angry, we want to *do* something about it. But getting mad about people or situations at school can be frustrating because we often can't change the things that make us angry. We can't fire the principal or write in better grades on our report cards. And we can't run away from problems at school because the law says we have to attend.**

Jesus was in a situation like that. If He was going to die on the cross for our sins, He couldn't wipe out everybody who irritated Him. He couldn't escape by running back to heaven either—not if He was going to fulfill His mission on earth. So let's look at how He handled anger, to see how we should handle ours.

EXPLORING THE WORD

JESUS AND ANGER

Assign individuals or teams to look up the following passages. They should prepare to tell the whole group what the verses say about (1) whether Jesus got angry, (2) why He got angry, and (3) how He showed His anger. As needed, supplement students' reports with the summaries in parentheses.

- **Mark 3:1-6** (Jesus wanted to heal a man who had a shriveled hand. He knew the religious leaders were watching, waiting for Him to break their rule about not doing anything on the day of rest. Jesus was furious because these hypocrites cared more about their rules than they did about helping the man. So He looked around at them with anger on His face, told the man to stretch out his hand, and healed him.)

- **Matthew 16:21-23** (Jesus did more than give an angry look this time. He said, "Get behind Me, Satan!" to Peter, who had just suggested that Jesus wouldn't be killed and raised from the dead. Jesus called Peter a stumbling block, which probably means that Peter was making it harder for Jesus to follow God's plan that required Him to die.)

- **John 2:13-17** (Jesus went to Jerusalem, where He found that dishonest businessmen had set up shop in the courts of the temple. Some of them were ripping people off by charging outrageous rates to change foreign money. Some were making money by selling animals to sacrifice. Jesus was angry that His Heavenly Father's house was being turned into a sort of crooked flea market—so angry that He charged in, shouting, and turned the money changers' tables over.)

- **Matthew 23:27-33** (This is part of an angry speech Jesus made to the religious leaders who were leading people astray. He let them have it, calling them hypocrites, unclean, wicked, descendants of murderers, and snakes—and said they were condemned to hell.)

- **Mark 15:2-5** (Jesus had been arrested, even though He was innocent. He was taken before Pilate and falsely accused of crimes, but He didn't defend Himself—even though He was about to be tortured and killed.)

Explain: **There are a lot of things we can learn from these verses about how Jesus handled anger. Here are some of them:**

1. **Jesus knew that feeling angry isn't wrong in itself. But He chose how He would respond to people and situations that angered Him. He didn't *always* turn over tables or call everybody "Satan." Sometimes He didn't say anything at all. Instead of letting anger control Him, *He* controlled *it*.**
2. **Jesus was slow to anger. He didn't make His angry speech to the religious leaders the first time they made Him mad. He didn't fly off the handle.**
3. **Jesus usually expressed anger instead of bottling it up. But He didn't do it in ways that hurt others unnecessarily. He didn't try to get even.**
4. **Jesus turned His anger to action in order to serve others, but not to defend Himself. He stood up for the man with the withered hand, for God, for those of us who would benefit from His death, and for those who were being led astray by the religious leaders. But when *He* was wronged, He left it to God to see that justice would be done.**
5. **Jesus' top priority was obeying God. It wasn't making sure that everybody treated Him fairly. When expressing His anger would have kept people from knowing God, He didn't try to change things or even gripe about them. He wants us to have the same attitude, even though it's not always easy. He knows we'll get angry sometimes, but He has shown us through His example how we can choose to respond.**

APPLYING THE TRUTH

WORKOUT SHEET

Distribute Workout Sheet # 8, "Letting Off Steam." If necessary, remind your students of the five principles you just presented. Then give them time to complete the sheet.

When the exercise is completed, have your young people share their answers. Don't worry if there's some disagreement; just ask how the answers square with Jesus' way of handling anger. Some of the answers will reflect differences in personality rather than morality. For example, one student may find that his anger dissipates when he jogs or rides his bike; another may say that exercise makes him madder.

STUDENT BOOK OPTION

Review the example of Laurie, who blew up at her friends for ruining her chances to be a cheerleader. Say: **Laurie may have been "justified" in blowing up, but why was she wrong?** (Her motive was to hurt and get revenge. She selfishly clung to her own rights. See Philippians 2:5-8.) **Laurie should also make sure that the girls' accusation that she was stuck-up isn't true.**

SUMMARY

Here are some general comments you may wish to make:

Arguing hardly ever makes us less angry; the more we try to make our point, the more angry we tend to get. The same is true of punching the wall; it hurts us *and* the wall. Fighting, name-calling, and trying to get even are all forms of revenge, and vengeance belongs only to God (Romans 12:19). Getting even may feel good for a minute, but can keep the other person from knowing God; how can we take revenge, then turn around and tell the person how God loves him? Punching a pillow is OK—unless you're pretending to punch the person who made you mad, which means you still have a "get even" attitude. Talking with a friend or parent can be helpful; just be careful that you're not trying to tear another person down without having to face him. Talking with the person who's the problem can be risky, but if you've calmed down first, have prayed about it, and don't insist that things turn out your way, it can help a lot. Jogging or other exercise helps many people burn off the adrenalin that charges through them when they get mad, and they feel better. Praying is the best solution of all—not because it "sounds spiritual," but because only God can change us, other people, and situations.

Close by putting that final advice into action—pray that God will give your students the patience and wisdom to handle anger-producers in a Christlike way at school this week.

PART TWO

Creatures from The School Zone

Your young teens face an assortment of strange beings at school—some stranger than others. There's the English teacher who uses the same lesson plans she used when Shakespeare was in her class; the coach who forbids his wrestlers to eat anything but vitamins for three months to keep them in the lowest possible weight categories; the ninth-grade bully who grabs seventh-graders and makes them sit on the water fountain; the "best friend" who stops talking to you if you wear the wrong flavor of lip gloss; and the non-Christian who breaks all the rules and gets all the rewards while you toe the line and get laughed at. Getting along with all these people would challenge the charm of Dale Carnegie—not to mention the social novices in your group.

But getting along in The School Zone is even more challenging—and rewarding—if your students do it Jesus' way. The following four sessions will show them what it means to treat teachers and principals, friends, enemies, and non-Christians in a Christlike fashion.

Be prepared to follow up on these sessions, especially if your students mention specific people at school with whom they don't get along. Ask about these people from time to time, and if possible, pray with students about teachers they see as unfair or students who intimidate them. By helping your young people build relationships with those at school, you'll grow closer to them as well.

CREATURES FROM THE SCHOOL ZONE

SESSION 5

NO MORE TEACHERS?

KEY CONCEPT

We can get along better with teachers and other school authorities when we recognize that God has placed them where they are.

MEETING THE NEED

This session will respond to student questions and comments like these:

- "One of my teachers is out to get me."
- "Our principal is a jerk."
- "My English teacher wants us to read a book with a lot of swearing in it. Do I have to?"

SESSION GOALS

You'll help each group member

1. identify his or her conflicts with school authorities,
2. see that God allows even "bad" teachers and principals to be in authority over us,
3. learn how to "render unto teachers" that which is theirs, and unto God that which is His.

SPECIAL PREPARATION

_____ If you play the "No-Name Game," bring the objects listed under that section of "Building the Body."

BUILDING THE BODY

Use one or both of these activities to suggest in an entertaining way that "no more teachers" may not be a very good idea.

NO-NAME GAME

Bring the following objects used for playing games: a golf ball, checkerboard (or other game board), Ping-Pong paddle, and egg timer. Tell the group that you've discovered a new game, and it uses all of these seemingly unrelated objects. But you're not going to tell them how the game is played; they have one minute to figure that out. Don't give them any hints until their time is up. If they haven't guessed the rules by then, you may want to give one or two vague hints and allow them another 30 seconds. They may come up with *a* game, but it probably won't be the right one. When time is called, explain that the object of the game is to hit the golf ball with the paddle so that it rolls through the "tunnel" (created by folding the game board in half and propping it up). When the ball rolls through, it's supposed to hit the egg timer. You can play a few rounds of the game if you like, but the point is to show the value of getting the right instructions. Make this point later in the lesson, explaining that teachers usually know more than students do about the rules of "life after school," and are needed to get us on the right track for the "game" we'll face later on.

TV TRIVIA TEST

Ask your students whether they'd rather do schoolwork or watch TV. Since many would probably rather watch TV, announce that you're going to give your group the kind of quiz they don't get in the classroom—a TV trivia test. Individuals or teams may compete as you ask the following questions (answers are in parentheses):

1. **What was Dr. McCoy's first name on *Star Trek*?** (Leonard)
2. **What color is a Smurf?** (Blue)
3. **What's the name of the car on *Knight Rider*?** (K.I.T.T.)
4. **What was Murdoch's nickname on *The A-Team*?** (Howlin' Mad)
5. **Which Muppet led his own band?** (Dr. Teeth)
6. **What's the occupation of Bill Cosby's wife on *The Cosby Show*?** (Lawyer)
7. **Who wrote the theme music for *Amazing Stories*?** (John Williams)
8. **What actress played Mallory on *Family Ties*?** (Justine Bateman)
9. **What company's commercial showed a lady who kept saying, "Where's the beef?"** (Wendy's)
10. **Who played the Six Million Dollar Man?** (Lee Majors)
11. **What color was the Incredible Hulk?** (Green)
12. **What game show was hosted by Richard Dawson?** (Family Feud)
13. **What's the nickname of the nerdy inventor on *Riptide*?** (The Boz)
14. **What was the number of the M.A.S.H. unit on *M.A.S.H.*?** (4077)

15. On *The Waltons,* what did John-Boy want to be when he grew up? (A writer)

After the quiz, explain that if we *always* watched TV instead of doing schoolwork, we would only know trivia like this—which wouldn't help us cope with the real world. We may not like having to learn what teachers and administrators want us to learn, but it's better than not knowing anything we can use.

LAUNCHING THE LESSON

WORKOUT SHEET

Distribute Workout Sheet #9, "Reverse Report Card." After giving your young teens time to fill it out, discuss their answers. Find out which traits they feel are most important in a good teacher and why. Ask whether there are any qualities they like to see in a teacher which are not listed on the sheet. Give them a chance to air their gripes about teachers they don't like, but don't let this part of the discussion go on for more than a few minutes; make sure it's balanced by students' descriptions of teachers they like. Then ask: **Which classes are you doing best in—the ones taught by favorite teachers or least favorite teachers?** (Most students will probably say they do best in favorite teachers' classes. If not, ask which classes they prefer to attend—those taught by favorite or least favorite teachers.) **Most of us tend to like classes which are taught by teachers we like. Sometimes liking the teacher helps us like the class; sometimes liking a subject helps us like the teacher. Either way, school is a lot easier to take when we get along with the teachers and administrators.**

But what happens when you get a teacher or principal you don't care for? What can you do? (Not much. You can't fire a teacher or principal. You usually can't switch to another class or school. You could talk with the teacher or principal about your complaints, but you'd still have to live with the results.) **What *do* you do if you get a teacher who lacks the qualities on the "report card" you just filled out?** (Tough it out, resent the teacher, complain to parents and friends, etc.)

Is it easier to do a big homework assignment for a teacher you like or for one you don't like? (It's usually easier for one we like.) **If we have a conflict with a teacher, it can actually be harder to learn in that class. If we think the teacher is boring, we have to try harder to listen. If we think the teacher is unfair, we may think it's pointless to study because we'll get a lower grade than we deserve anyway. So not getting along with teachers can affect our report cards as well as our emotions.**

How about the principal and the other people who make the rules at your school? On a scale of one to ten, how fair do you think they are? (Wait for an answer, and ask for elaboration.) **If you've ever been called into the principal's office for being in a fight or breaking a dress code or talking back to a teacher, you know how it can affect the way you feel about the whole school.** (Ask whether your students have ever been in trouble at school and how they felt.)

If you start to feel like "the system" is out to get you or doesn't care about you, just *going* to school can be hard. Some students drop out to get away from the people in charge, but they discover there are plenty of other authorities waiting for them in the outside world—like the police, bosses, and the government. If we can figure out how God wants us to treat all these people in charge, our lives at school can be a lot easier.

STUDENT BOOK OPTION

Ask: **What happened when Greg "wished away" all the school authorities?** (Everything was in a state of havoc, and his life was miserable.) **Why did Greg prefer, in the end, having authorities over him?** (They created order and protected him.)

EXPLORING THE WORD

WORKOUT SHEET

Hand out copies of Workout Sheet #10, "True or False?" Since answering the questions requires looking up quite a few verses, you may want to allow students to work in teams of three or four. When you regather the group, go through the answers so that students can grade their papers. Answers are as follows: (1) T; (2) F; (3) T; (4) F; (5) F; (6) F; (7) T; (8) T; (9) T; (10) F; (11) F: (12) T; (13) T; (14) F; (15) F.

Then go through the answers again, this time asking what each passage has to tell us about getting along with teachers, principals, and other authorities. As needed, use the following comments (numbered to correspond with the Workout Sheet) to supplement your young people's answers:

1. ***Jesus thought learning was worthwhile.* In His day, Jewish boys were taught the Scriptures starting at age five. At age twelve, they were expected to obey God's Word as grown-ups. That was when Jesus went to the temple and amazed the teachers. He had obviously been paying attention in class. We can learn something else from this passage too: *Jesus wasn't afraid to talk with the authorities.* Can you imagine going to the nearest university and discussing geometry or literature with the professors? Jesus was younger than most junior high students when He went to the temple, but that didn't stop Him. We don't have to be afraid to talk with our teachers or principals either, and talking can help if we have conflicts with them.**

2. ***Jesus kept learning as He grew up.* He didn't say, "Well, I'm such a genius that I amazed those teachers at the temple," and coast from then on. He grew in wisdom and in favor with others.**

3. ***Jesus went to "class" regularly, even though it could have bored Him.* If anyone knew the Scriptures, it was Jesus. But He kept going to the synagogue on the Sabbath. We tend to decide right away whether a teacher or class is going to be**

boring, then skip out mentally or physically.

4. *Jesus opposed the "experts" when they opposed the truth.* He listened to them and learned from them as He grew up, but when the time came He wasn't afraid to disagree with them. We are to listen and learn too, and respect our teachers, but we don't have to cringe quietly in a corner if they teach something that opposes God's Word. We can speak up—if we know for sure what the truth is, and can say it in a way that doesn't drive that teacher further from God.

5. *We can't use our faith as an excuse for not obeying our teachers and principals.* Unless they're telling us to do something that is clearly wrong, we're to give them what they ask for (including homework and obedience to school rules).

6. *Violence against teachers (and others) is wrong.* Some students have beaten, stabbed, or shot teachers they had grudges against. Jesus' example showed that striking back is not allowed.

7. *God puts people in authority over us.* This can be hard to swallow, especially if we have unfair or hostile teachers or principals. But when the Apostle Paul wrote this, the government was far worse than our school administrators; the Romans were putting Christians to death. Yet God was in charge and allowed the Romans to have authority.

8. *Rebellion goes right to the top.* Since God is in charge, we're fighting Him if we rebel at school—unless we're rebelling against having to do something the Bible prohibits.

9. *The authorities are there to protect us.* It may not seem that way at times, but the people who run our schools are there for our good. Imagine how hard it would be to learn if all the teachers and principals suddenly disappeared. How safe would you feel in the halls?

10. *Obey because it's right.* Anybody can follow the rules just to keep from being expelled. Christians obey to please God.

11. *Obey on the inside too.* You can fool your teachers, but you can't fool God. He sees whether you're rebelling inside.

12. *Your real "boss" is God.* When it's hard to do what teachers and principals say because they're tough to get along with, remember that you're really working for the Lord. Do it for Him.

13. *God's Word is the final authority.* If you think you're being told to do something wrong, check with a parent or pastor who can help you find out what the Bible says. In a disagreement between God and man, God wins.

14. *Every teacher or other person in charge is to be respected.* It doesn't matter whether he or she "deserves" it. And being mistreated isn't an excuse for being disrespectful.

15. ***Don't slack off if you go to a Christian school.*** **Christian teachers and principals deserve your best. Whether you're in a public or private school, don't try to get away with more in a Christian teacher's class.**

APPLYING THE TRUTH

A CLOSER LOOK

Have students look at Workout Sheet #9, "Reverse Report Card," again. They should think about the teachers they chose as "least favorite." Ask how much your young people know about these teachers' private lives, the pressures they may face. Have they ever considered what it's like to be a teacher or principal? What would be hardest about these jobs? What authorities do teachers and principals have to obey? (School boards, superintendents, government agencies, God.) The object is to encourage students to think of school authority figures as real people with problems—who must also submit to those "above" them.

Discuss which of the truths listed under "Exploring the Word" will be most difficult for your students to obey this week. How would their attitudes have to change in order to see their least favorite teachers as appointed by God? Have your young people close in audible or silent prayer for their least favorite teachers, and for their own need to help, learn from, and obey all of their teachers and administrators.

CREATURES FROM THE SCHOOL ZONE

SESSION 6

WITH FRIENDS LIKE THESE . . .

KEY CONCEPT

Making and keeping friends at school is easier when we meet and treat them as Jesus did.

MEETING THE NEED

In this session, you'll respond to student questions and comments like these:

- "I don't have any friends at school."
- "This person and I used to be friends, but we're not speaking to each other anymore."
- "How can I get people to like me?"

SESSION GOALS

You'll help each group member

1. identify the qualities that make a good friend,
2. discover how Jesus met and treated His friends,
3. explore ways to put Jesus' friendship principles into action at school.

SPECIAL PREPARATION

_____ If you plan to use the "Building the Body" activity called "Closer Than You Think," bring enough pencils and paper for the whole group.

_____ If you wish to award prizes for games, bring those too.

_____ Don't forget light refreshments if you plan a "friendly" social time at the end.

BUILDING THE BODY

Try one or more of these games to bring your students together in a friendly but nonthreatening way.

SHY CHARADES

Each of your students is to tell the whole group something about himself or herself (place of birth, favorite hobby, favorite food, most disliked spot for a vacation, career goal, etc.). But the information must be acted out, not spoken. Each person may choose and announce the category (favorite musical group, etc.), but the rest is to be communicated through gestures only. Whoever guesses the most information wins. After the game, point out that making friends requires getting to know each other—and that's extra hard if we're too shy to share information about ourselves. Making friends takes longer if we force others to guess what we're really like.

CLOSER THAN YOU THINK

Divide the group into relatively unfamiliar pairs as you count off by twos. Then explain that most friends like to have something in common, and you want your group members to know how much alike they really are. Pass out paper and a pencil to each pair and tell them that they have one minute to list everything they have in common as a pair. The lists can include anything *except* the fact that both students go to the same church. Whichever pair lists the most commonalities within the time limit wins.

SECRET HANDSHAKE

Have your group stand in a circle. As the leader, you start things off by shaking hands with the person to your right. That person must shake hands with the person to his right, but in doing so has to add a movement or noise (such as snapping the fingers, bumping elbows, sneezing, etc.). The more complicated handshake is then passed further to the right, where another twist is added. The process continues around the circle, the handshake becoming increasingly complex, until someone misses one of the movements or noises. That person is then out of the game, and the process starts anew with the next player. Continue the game until you're down to one person, or until you're able to get all the way around the circle without a mistake (whichever is shorter). Later in the lesson, recall this game as an illustration of how much harder it is to make and keep friends when we demand too much of them.

LAUNCHING THE LESSON

WORKOUT SHEET

Distribute Workout Sheet #11, "Frankenfriend." As you do so, set the scene of the mad doctor's dungeon laboratory by saying in an eerie voice (as much like Boris Karloff's as you can manage): **And now, my friends, you are about to undertake an experiment. You're deep in a Transylvanian castle, and the lightning is flashing all around you . . . and you are about to create . . . Frankenfriend!** Allow your students time to complete their sheets, encouraging them to give answers that truly reflect what they would look for in the ideal friend.

When you regroup to discuss the exercise, ask volunteers to share some of their answers. Some will be flip, others revealing. Then ask: **Which of these is more important to you in a friend: (1) clothing style or sympathy? (2) body or brains? (3) humor or money? (4) popularity or loyalty? (5) faith or personality? (6) talent or smile?** (Allow time after each question for your young teens to think and answer. Some of the choices may not be easy for them, and it's better to get an honest answer than a "pat" one. For example, would they *really* rather have a dull Christian friend instead of a non-Christian one with lots of personality? Point out that in real life the choices are not so clear-cut. But we do tend to accept or reject people quickly on the basis of looks and popularity—rather than waiting to find out whether they have qualities like sympathy and loyalty.)

Continue to discuss the Workout Sheet by asking: **In what ways would you want your ideal friend to be like you?** (Answers will probably revolve around having common interests, hobbies, tastes in entertainment, faith, etc.) **In what ways would you want him or her to be the exact *opposite* of you?** (This one may be harder for your students to answer, so you may have to suggest responses and ask whether they ring true. Do your young people want friends of the opposite sex? Friends with different interests that would broaden their horizons? Friends whose strengths make up for their own perceived weaknesses—such as a quiet person who wants an outgoing friend to be his "front man," or a "jock" who wants the class brain to help him with homework? Or do your students see traits in themselves, such as stubbornness, which they couldn't stand in someone else?)

Say: **Creating an ideal friend like "Frankenfriend" is OK as an exercise, but real life doesn't work that way. We don't get to build our friends from scratch. That means they may have traits we don't like as well as some we do. In other words, they're imperfect—just like we are. And who would want a homemade friend anyway? He'd only like you because he had no choice. We want people to choose to be our friends, to like us for who and what we are.**

STUDENT BOOK OPTION

Ask: **How did Betsy McMegabuddy make 523 "friends"?** (She fit the mold she thought people liked; handed out money; used "clever" conversation.) **Were these friendships real?** (No. People probably just used Betsy to get what they wanted.)

Making and keeping friends at school is harder for some people than others, but we all need help with it. That's why we're going to check out how Jesus met people and treated friends. We can't change other people into ideal friends or force them to like us, but if we follow Jesus' example, we'll be the kind of people others will want as friends.

EXPLORING THE WORD

JESUS' APPROACH

Lead into your Bible study by asking students which of the following they consider to be the hardest part of making friends: (1) not knowing whether others will like them; (2) getting up the courage to approach kids they don't know; (3) thinking of something to say; (4) finding a way into a clique or group; or (5) finding kids at school who meet their own "friendship standards." Discuss their choices, encouraging students to share a couple of experiences in which they made friends—or failed to make them. Then have one or more volunteers read John 4:1-15 aloud. Follow the reading with questions and comments like these:

We can learn a few things from this story about how Jesus approached people and got to know them. First of all, how worried did Jesus seem about whether the woman would like Him? (Not worried at all.) **Jesus never seemed to worry about whether people liked Him, yet He made a lot of friends. He knew He had something to offer people. What was it?** (Living water—salvation.) **We can tell people about salvation too if we've received Christ as Saviour. But besides that, each of us has something special to offer other people—*ourselves.* Nobody else can be exactly the kind of friend you can be. If you spend all your time worrying about whether people will like you, you'll never get to find out.**

Did Jesus have to work hard to get His courage up to talk to the woman? (Apparently not.) **Why not?** (It was natural; He was thirsty and needed a drink.) **It's a lot easier to approach people if we don't make a big deal of it. Jesus didn't run behind a bush and comb His hair or make sure He was wearing the right sandals before He could meet anybody. If you want to make friends, try getting involved in an informal activity where it's natural to talk—and be yourself.**

What amazing, wise, witty thing did Jesus say first to impress the woman? ("Will you give Me a drink?") **Isn't that great? We could never think of anything that clever, could we? Jesus didn't worry about coming up with a speech to "break the ice." He just said something that was natural and logical in the situation. We worry about whether our voices will crack, or whether we'll forget what we rehearsed in our minds. Try talking normally and see what happens.**

Jesus was Jewish; the woman was Samaritan. Those were two very exclusive "cliques" that had nothing to do with each other. They disagreed on just about everything religious. So what did Jesus talk about? (Water.) **Who could disagree about water? He used something they had in common to make a point about faith in God. To make**

friends, find out what *other* people are interested in; then see what you have in common. That doesn't mean you give up who you are and imitate them. Jesus didn't *become* a Samaritan; He built a bridge to one.**

By Jewish standards at that time, no Samaritan was fit to be a friend. And men and women who were strangers weren't supposed to talk to each other. Did Jesus seem concerned about that? (No.) **He didn't just talk to people He thought would make ideal friends; He got to know people who *needed* friends. If you want to make friends, you'll make more if you don't write off those who need friends as much as you do.**

WORKOUT SHEET

Now let's look at how Jesus wants us to treat friends once we have them. Distribute Workout Sheet #12, "The Best of Friends." Give students time to look up the five passages and complete the sentences. Then discuss their answers, using the following summaries as needed.

1. **John 11:31-36** (Jesus showed how much He cared for His friend Lazarus by raising him from the dead, but what first impressed bystanders was the fact that Jesus cried over His friend's death. Are we willing to let our friends know—while they're still alive—how we feel about them? Jesus wasn't embarrassed or afraid to show emotion, and sometimes our friends need to hear from us that we care.)

2. **John 13:34-35** (Jesus said we should love each other as He loves us. He loves us unconditionally, which means without strings; unselfishly, because He gave everything for us; and always, no matter where we move or whether we make a mistake. Jesus' love is perfect, which is more than we can say for most of our friendships. We usually want to meet people halfway, giving no more than they do. But Jesus loved us 100 percent, even when we didn't know Him.)

3. **John 13:1-5, 14-16** (Jesus showed how friends should act toward each other by washing His disciples' feet. That was a way of being humble, doing the "dirty work" in order to meet another person's need. Jesus didn't use His friends for whatever He could get out of them; He served them. The more interested we are in meeting other people's needs, the less phony our friendships will be—and the more friends we'll probably have.)

4. **John 15:13** (Jesus said friends should be willing to lay down their lives for each other. This usually doesn't mean having to die for someone else, though it did for Jesus; for us it means *living* our lives for others. If we're not willing to give anything up for our friends, our "friendships" are based on getting instead of caring.)

5. **Matthew 26:56; 28:8-10, 16-20** (After Jesus' friends deserted Him, He responded by forgiving them and letting them come back. He even sought them out. True friends don't hold grudges or keep track of how many times they've been wronged. Peter denied three times that he even *knew* Jesus, yet Jesus forgave him. Are we willing to forgive our friends if they make us mad? Or do we give them the silent treatment, or go around saying mean things about them?)

APPLYING THE TRUTH

ROLE PLAY

Divide your students into "casts" to role play the following situations for the rest of the group. Give them a minute or two to plan their skits, which should show how Jesus might want them to meet and treat friends.

1. Your best friend tells several other kids your deepest secret—that you have a crush on someone of the opposite sex in your science class. Your name starts appearing with that someone's in "true love" valentine shapes on the chalkboard, and your friend just laughs. What do you do when you see your friend after school?

2. You're new at school and don't know anybody. In the lunchroom you sit with a group of kids who appear to be friends with each other. What do you do? If you're part of the group of friends and notice the new person, what do you do?

3. You've been friends with another person since third grade. You're both Christians; you've had a lot of good times together; you've helped each other with work and problems too. Now your friend is feeling down and says, "Nobody really likes me. I'm no good at anything. You probably let me hang around because you feel sorry for me." What do you do?

After each role play, applaud the participants. Discuss how well the characters followed Jesus' model of making and keeping friends. What could they have done differently? If possible, end the session by serving light refreshments and encouraging students to get to know a little more about each other in this informal, friendly atmosphere.

CREATURES FROM THE SCHOOL ZONE

SESSION 7

. . . WHO NEEDS ENEMIES?

KEY CONCEPT

Loving our enemies at school may not be easy, but it's Jesus' way—and can lead to rewards now and later.

MEETING THE NEED

This session will respond to student concerns like these:

- "Most of the white kids at school hate me for being black. What am I supposed to do?"
- "If somebody else starts a fight, can't I just fight back?"
- "I don't go around hitting people I don't like. Isn't that enough?"

SESSION GOALS

You'll help each group member

1. see that hiding and fighting don't make enemies go away,
2. examine Jesus' treatment of enemies,
3. think of ways to put into practice Jesus' commands to "love your enemies" and to be peacemakers.

SPECIAL PREPARATION

_____ If you want to award prizes in "Malicious Matchup" (a "Building the Body" activity), bring some.

BUILDING THE BODY

Try Workout Sheet #13 and/or the exercise "Name-calling" to get your group thinking about enemies.

WORKOUT SHEET

Distribute Workout Sheet #13, "Public Enemies Number One." Have your students match up these real and fictional antagonists. Here are the answers: (1-H; 2-K; 3-I; 4-N; 5-A; 6-L; 7-M; 8-C; 9-O; 10-D; 11-B; 12-J; 13-G; 14-E; 15-F). If desired, award a prize for the first student to get all the answers correct.

NAME-CALLING

Divide the group into two teams and have them stand on opposite sides of the room. Team A is "The Insult Infantry"; Team B is "The Blessing Battalion." Team A is to hurl an insult at Team B, indicating how dumb Team B is. Team B is to respond by calling out a *compliment* to Team A, describing how *smart* Team A is. Let this insult/blessing process continue for a minute or so; then have the teams reverse roles. After another minute or so, have both teams send compliments to one another about how good-looking, intelligent, and well-dressed they are.

Both teams will probably run out of compliments pretty quickly. When they do (or when it's time to move on), ask both teams which was harder to make up—insults or blessings. (Probably blessings.) Which felt more satisfying to send? (Probably insults.) Which felt more awkward? (Probably blessings.) Which are we more used to throwing at each other? (Probably insults.) Which do your students think God wants them to give each other? (Probably blessings.) Point out that even though we know it's not right, we'd usually rather put people down than give them compliments. And if it's hard to compliment a friend, it's even harder to bless an enemy.

LAUNCHING THE LESSON

GETTING ALONG

Say: **OK, let's have everybody who likes every person at school—every student, every teacher, the principal, the janitor—if you like *everybody, every day,* stand up.** (A few may stand, but probably not many.) **Now let's have everybody who is *liked* by everyone else at school—always liked by every student, teacher, and cook in the cafeteria—stand up.** (A few misinformed individuals might stand, but the rest will probably set them straight. Before continuing, congratulate any who have stood and let them sit down.) **This lesson is only for people who don't always get along with everyone at school. Some of you may think you get along with everybody, but now the rest of us don't get**

along with *you* because you're so perfect—so you'll have to stay and listen too.

Those of you who didn't stand up, tell us—who are some of these people at school with whom you don't always get along too well? (Wait for answers. If your young teens are reluctant to go into detail, refer to the following partial list of possibilities to jog their memories:

- The guy who always makes fun of you in P.E. class because you can't do as many push-ups as he can;
- The "teacher's pet" who does everything right and makes you look bad;
- The kids who accuse you of *being* the teacher's pet because you get good grades and aren't rowdy in class;
- The kid who keeps telling you to meet him after school so he can beat your head in—to prove you're not "chicken";
- The kids who give you a hard time for being a Christian, not being a Christian, wearing glasses, not wearing glasses, being black, being white, or being whatever else they don't happen to be;
- The former friend who decided one day that she didn't like you all that much anymore, started hanging around with somebody else, and tells everybody that you have bad breath and a contagious disease.)

Say: **School enemies usually fall into one of these categories:**

1. **People who like to see whether they can make us mad, or get others to dislike us or laugh at us;**
2. **People who like to see whether they can scare us;**
3. **People who keep us from getting things we deserve;**
4. **People who physically hurt us or steal from us;**
5. **People who betray us, who let us down.**

STUDENT BOOK OPTION

What are typical TV solutions to problems with enemies? (Revenge, violence, put-downs, etc.) **Are these really solutions?** (No, they don't solve anything. People still remain enemies.)

THE ENEMY

Now, let's find out how you deal with your enemies. Let's have you stand up if you can point your finger at an enemy and blast him off the face of the earth with a lightning bolt. (If somebody stands up, tell him he has to demonstrate his amazing power or sit down.) **OK, stand up if you can just snap your fingers and make your enemies disappear.** (Use same reply as before.) **Well, then, how *do* you deal with people at school who cause you trouble?** (Fight them, ignore them, run from them, stay out of their way, get back at them, etc.) **Are there any problems with fighting your enemies?** (You can get in trouble; you can lose; even if you win, they will probably still be your enemies and may try to get back at you.) **Are there any problems with running from your enemies or hiding from them?** (They might find you; you might worry all the time about whether they'll find you; you may feel like a failure for not facing them.) **If you**

want to fight or hide for the rest of your years in school—and the rest of your life—that's up to you. But there's a better way. It's not necessarily an *easier* way, but it solves more problems than fighting or hiding. It's the way Jesus used, and we're going to find out about it.

EXPLORING THE WORD

Read the following "enemies list," asking what your students would feel like doing if they had school enemies like these:

1. Kids who make fun of you because you're different;
2. Teachers who call you a liar and try to have you thrown out;
3. A person who pretends to be your best friend and then has you arrested for something you didn't do;
4. A bully who spits in your face, hits you until you're bleeding, and then turns you over to someone else who's ready to kill you.

JESUS' ENEMIES

After students answer, say: **Jesus had enemies like all of these. His brothers thought He was strange; the religious teachers wanted to throw Him out of the synagogue and have Him killed; His so-called friend Judas betrayed Him to His enemies who came to arrest Him; and the soldiers beat Him, spat on Him, and nailed Him to a cross.**

Have one or more of your young teens read aloud Matthew 26:14-25, 45-50. Before the reading begins, ask the rest of the students to raise their hands during the story whenever they think Jesus could have fought or run away from Judas if He'd wanted to. After the passage is read, point out that since Jesus knew Judas was going to betray Him, He could have fought or run away from Judas at any time—but didn't. In fact, He even called Judas "friend" when Judas came to betray Him. Explain: **Jesus didn't fight or run from His enemies. Unlike us, He could have destroyed His enemies with lightning bolts or made them disappear with a snap of His fingers. But He didn't. In fact, He didn't even *hate* them. But there *were* a few things He did to His enemies, and He wants us to do them too.**

WORKOUT SHEET

Distribute Workout Sheet #14, "New, Old Sayings." Explain that the sayings on the left side of the sheet express most people's feelings about how to deal with enemies. The Bible verses on the right side show what Jesus taught instead. Have your students look up the passages and write Jesus' "new sayings" in their own words. When they're finished, ask them to share their answers and tell why it would be easy or hard for them to obey what Jesus taught. As needed, use the following summaries to supplement students' answers:

1. ***Settle matters quickly with your adversary.* Don't hold a grudge against your enemy. Don't let him *stay* your enemy a minute**

longer than you have to. This can be hard if your enemy refuses to talk with you; more often, though, it's hard because we like to hold onto our angry feelings, think about how bad our enemies are and how good we are, and tell everybody else who will listen.

2. *Do to others as you would have them do to you.* This doesn't mean we should always do what others want us to do; it means we should treat people—even enemies—as we'd want them to treat us. This is hard because we think enemies don't deserve to be treated as well as we do. But Jesus didn't say anything about deserving. He just said *do.*

3. *Don't resist an evil person; turn the other cheek.* This sounds absolutely crazy to most people. A lot of the shows on TV would have to go off the air if their characters couldn't hit or shoot or blow up their enemies anymore; people would say they were too wimpy or boring. But Jesus practiced this saying as well as the others. It takes two to fight, and if one refuses, the fight will probably be a lot shorter.

4. *Do good to those who hate you; bless those who curse you.* It's not enough, according to Jesus, to refuse to hit back. We're actually supposed to help enemies who hate us and say nice things to those who call us names or swear at us. We can do this only when we remember how God sent Jesus to help people who hated Him. And even then it takes practice.

5. *Love your enemies and pray for them.* We can fake the rest—even saying nice things to our enemies—but we need to ask God for His love before we can really love those who mistreat us. That means seeing our enemies as God does—as people who need love. And why should we pray for our enemies? Because only God can change them.

6. *Forgive your enemies.* We may not feel like doing this. But if we don't forgive, why should God forgive *our* sins? And if God can forgive our enemies, who are we to say they're too bad for *us* to forgive?

7. *Keep forgiving.* Sure, we can forgive once or twice. But can we forgive seventy times seven (or seventy-seven, depending on your version)? The same person, calling us the same names or letting us down in the same way? The same teacher, grading us down again and again for some unknown reason? Yes, says Jesus—we can forgive, just as God keeps forgiving us.

8. *Be a peacemaker.* When you have a choice, do the thing that leads to peace. It may mean not having your way. It may mean not saying that great insult you think up when somebody's giving you a hard time. But just as Jesus had to put up with insults and death to make peace between us and God, we can choose not to play an enemy's game.

9. *Do even more for an enemy than he demands of you.* This is hard too, but it sometimes surprises an enemy so much that he feels too ashamed to demand any more of you.

10. ***Love your enemies and God will reward you.*** **Will He reward you right away? Not necessarily. You may have to wait until you get to heaven. But even now you'll be more like your Heavenly Father because He is kind to people (like us) who don't deserve it.**

APPLYING THE TRUTH

CHOOSE ONE

Your young teens may give mental assent to these hard-to-obey teachings of Jesus as you explain them, but many will forget or ignore them in the stark reality of school. Point out the need to *choose* to follow Jesus in dealing with enemies; it doesn't automatically happen. Toward this end, have your students circle the sayings on Workout Sheet #14 which they honestly feel God wants them to obey. Then ask them to choose just *one* of Jesus' listed teachings which they will put into practice this week at school. Have them bow their heads and think of specific "enemies" at school to whom they could apply the command they've picked. Conclude by asking students to pray silently or aloud for these people who cause them problems, and for the strength to refuse to fight or run when confronted by enemies at school.

CREATURES FROM THE SCHOOL ZONE

SESSION 8

YOU'VE GOT A SECRET

KEY CONCEPT

Instead of avoiding, envying, or looking down on the non-Christians at school, we should care about them as Jesus did.

MEETING THE NEED

You'll respond in this session to student comments and questions like these:

- "I feel guilty because I don't tell other kids I'm a Christian."
- "Why bother to be a Christian? The non-Christian kids get to do anything they want."
- "I don't have anything in common with the non-Christians at school. Can't I just hang around with Christians?"

SESSION GOALS

You'll help each member of the group

1. become aware of those at school who need to meet Jesus,
2. learn how Jesus treated sinners,
3. see that witnessing is a way to show love to non-Christians at school.

SPECIAL PREPARATION

_____ If you plan to use the opener called "Newspaper Nobodies," find and bring the two newspaper articles as described under "Building the Body."

_____ If you want to try the "Telepathy Test," bring about a dozen index cards on which you've written numbers or letters, or drawn simple shapes.

_____ Practice reading the story, "The Witness," which appears in the lesson under "Applying the Truth."

BUILDING THE BODY

NEWSPAPER NOBODIES

During the week, clip two short articles from a newspaper. Each should be an account of an individual's achievement, crime, or misfortune. In one article—preferably the more sensational one—change the newsworthy person's name to that of one of your group members. Leave the other story as is. When you bring the clippings to class, announce that you have some news. Read the unchanged article first; note your students' response, which will probably be, "So what?" Then read the altered article about your group member. When your students react with greater interest (and laughter, if you've chosen a crime story), ask why they were more interested in the second clipping. They'll probably say it was because they knew the person involved. Mention that we usually care more about people we know personally. Later in the lesson, use this as an illustration of why it's important to see non-Christians at school as individuals, not a faceless "them," if we're going to care about them as Jesus did.

TELEPATHY TEST

Bring about a dozen index cards on which you've written easily recognizable symbols (numbers, letters, geometric shapes, etc.). Divide your group into pairs. Have each pair take a turn sitting in front of the group, with one member holding a card and trying to "project" its symbol into his partner's mind. The "mind-reading" partner must guess the symbol. Keep track of how many pairs prove to be "telepathic." The success rate will probably be miserable, which will enable you to point out that "ESP" and mind reading don't work. If we want a person to know something, we have to tell him or her. It's the same way with our faith—we can't expect non-Christians at school to read our minds and find out about Jesus. We have to tell them.

LAUNCHING THE LESSON

WORKOUT SHEET

Distribute Workout Sheet #15, "How Many?" As you do so, explain that you're taking a survey to find out about the schools represented in your group. Students may say they can't answer all the questions because they can't know for sure which kids and teachers are Christians—but for purposes of the sheet, their guesses and impressions are more important than statistical accuracy. You may want to take this opportunity to explain what a Christian really is, in case some of your young teens aren't sure. Point out that a true Christian is one who trusts Christ as his or her Saviour and seeks to follow Him as Lord; one becomes a Christian by admitting his own sinfulness to God, asking forgiveness, and believing that the death of God's Son, Jesus, pays for that sin.

After your students have completed the survey, have them share their answers. If more than one school is represented in your group, compare impressions of them. Pay special attention to what your young people reveal about their relationships with and feelings toward non-Christians (questions 2, 5-8). Do they seem to avoid or envy non-Christians? Do they feel guilty or fearful regarding witnessing? Rather than exhorting them at this point, ask about the sources of these feelings.

YOUR CHOICES

Then say: **Whether you go to a public school or a Christian school, you probably run into at least *some* non-Christians every day. You can:**

- **Ignore them and hang out only with Christians;**
- **Look down on them because they do things you don't like—such as swearing, drinking, using drugs, or making fun of Christians—or just because they don't care about God;**
- **Wish you could be like them because they don't have to go to church or pray or read the Bible or worry about witnessing, or because they get to do or buy things you can't;**
- **Feel sorry for them, but not do anything about it;**
- **Feel guilty because even though you figure you should tell them about Jesus, you don't because you think they'd laugh or say you were weird; or**
- **Drive them all crazy by hitting them over the head with your Bible and telling them they have to get saved right away.**

So how do you vote? Do you want to look down your nose, feel jealous, feel guilty, or drive everybody nuts? (Take a vote. Most of your students will probably abstain.)

If you are using the student books, review the author's experiences with witnessing to his school friends. Ask group members to identify in their minds friends of theirs who don't know Christ.

Well, maybe there *is* another way to treat non-Christians at school. Let's look at what Jesus did.

EXPLORING THE WORD

JESUS' CHOICE

Assign students to read the following verses aloud. After each passage is read, ask what it has to say about Jesus' attitudes and actions toward unbelievers. Use the summaries as needed.

Matthew 9:10-13 (Jesus had dinner at Matthew's house; Matthew was a tax collector, a person who was usually hated because most tax collectors at that time ripped people off by collecting more than they were supposed to. The religious teachers called the people at the dinner "sinners," and said Jesus should stay away from them. Matthew and his friends *were* sinners—but so were the Pharisees, and so are we. Jesus pointed out that these people needed help. They were spiritually sick, and He was like a doctor.)

Matthew 9:35-38 (Jesus went wherever people needed Him, helping them in two ways—preaching the Good News of the kingdom, which was that the Messiah had come, and healing those with all kinds of sickness. Think of all the diseased people Jesus touched; nobody was too dirty or smelly to be helped. When He looked at all those people, He had compassion on them, which means He cared enough to do something. He saw them as sheep without a shepherd, helpless and hassled.)

Luke 19:41-44 (Jesus came to a place overlooking Jerusalem, the city where He would eventually be tortured and killed. Instead of getting angry at the people for rejecting Him, He started to cry. He wished they would accept Him so that He could bring them peace, but He knew they were headed for destruction. He didn't say, "It'll serve these people right to be punished for what they'll do to Me." He cared about them enough to cry for them as well as die for them.)

John 8:10-11 (Even though He loved sinners, Jesus didn't love sin. He didn't say, "Since you're such a nice bunch of people, go ahead and do whatever you want." He told the woman who had been caught sinning that He didn't want to condemn her to death—but that she had to stop her sin.)

Hebrews 4:15 (Jesus spent a lot of time with sinners, but He didn't sin—ever. He was there to help people out of their sins, not to get dragged down with them.)

John 14:6 (Jesus took a stand when it came to the question of how to get to heaven. He could have said, "Hey, take any door you want." But He said He was the *only* way, whether people liked it or not. A lot of people didn't like it, and still don't, but He's still the only way.)

Say: **Jesus didn't avoid unbelievers; He was surrounded by them all the time. He didn't look down on them; He cared about them. He cried when He thought about how their unbelief would cause them to be punished. He didn't excuse or envy or imitate them, though; He knew that life without God may look good for awhile but in the end leads to being without God forever. That's why He came to earth, to provide a way to God—the only way. He wasn't afraid to let people know it either. He wanted them to be able to live with Him in heaven forever—because He loved them.**

Ask whether any of your students can quote John 3:16. If so, have one do it. Then appoint another to look up and read aloud John 3:16-17. Ask what these verses say about why God sent Jesus into the world (because He loved us; to give eternal life to anyone who believes in Him; not to condemn the world, but to save it). Explain that this is why Jesus sends us to school with the Good News about Him—because He loves the non-Christians there. When we start to see the people at school as He does, we'll find ourselves wanting to tell them about Him—in a natural way, not hitting them over the head, and because we care, not because we feel guilty.

APPLYING THE TRUTH

Your young teens may agree that they should witness at school, but they may not realize that they already *are* witnesses (in the sense of having witnessed, or seen, what it's like to know Jesus). Have a student read Acts 1:8, and explain that witness isn't just something you *do;* it's something you *are.* To bring home this point, read the following parable aloud.

THE WITNESS

Let's say you're standing on a street corner, and you see a red Corvette come screaming through the stop sign and plow into an old, gray Nova. Two minutes later a policeman comes by and asks you whether you saw what happened. Here's what you say:

"Oh, hi, Officer. Yeah, I saw the whole thing. It was really a mess—a wonder nobody got killed. What's that? You want me to be a what? A *witness?* Oh, man, no way! I mean, I can't witness. Witnessing's for other people. You know, people who have a way with words.

"You say I'm the only one who saw the accident? Well, there must be lots of other people who've seen accidents *somewhere.* Let *them* get up on the witness stand and tell about *their* accidents. Wouldn't that be just as good? No? Well, this accident wasn't all that spectacular. Get one of those other guys to testify—one who's seen a high-speed chase or a freeway pileup. Nobody would be interested in *my* story.

"See, I can't witness because I freeze up when I talk to groups. You need my cousin Arnold; he's taken a class in public speaking. What? Well, of course he didn't see the accident. But he's a great speaker!

"Aw, come on. I'm really busy; I can't take time to testify. And people would make fun of me. Maybe they'd disagree with me. What? You say that's not important, that I should just tell my story because I know it better than anyone else? But I don't know any of that *technical* stuff. I haven't even memorized any lines from the Driver's Manual! I haven't taken Driver Education!

"What? You say I'm an *expert?* An expert on what happened because I was the only guy who saw it? Yeah, but that doesn't make me a *witness,* does it? Isn't a witness somebody who tells about something?

"Huh? I already *am* a witness? You say a witness is somebody who witnesses—*sees*—something? So when I witnessed the accident, I became a witness? Uh-oh. That means it's just up to me to decide what *kind* of witness I want to be: one who's ready to tell what he's seen and heard, or one who isn't."

If we've received Christ as Saviour, we already *are* witnesses. We know what's happened to us. We've *witnessed* it. Once we realize that, and once we care about the non-Christians at school as Jesus does, we need to be ready to tell what we know when God gives us opportunities to talk with people. It helps if you think in advance about what's happened to you, maybe even writing it down to make it easier to remember. We're going to try a little of that today.

WORKOUT SHEET

Distribute Workout Sheet #16, "Your Story, Your Way." Have your students fill it out; fill one out yourself as well. Make the assignment as nonthreatening as possible by saying that it's OK if students can't remember an exact time when they received Christ and that they won't have to share their stories with the group unless they want to. When students are ready, start voluntary sharing of answers by telling your own. After as many students as possible have told their stories, urge them to take their sheets home and add details if more come to mind.

Be sensitive to the possibility that some of your group members may not know Christ; if the assignment confronts them with that fact, you may want to ask them after class how they felt about the stories. An opportunity for *you* to present the Gospel may arise. Close the session with prayer for the non-Christians at school, and for the love and courage to help them as Jesus did.

Winning in The School Zone

PART THREE

Loser. It's a title nobody wants, especially in The School Zone. The overachievers in your group are struggling to avoid the title by gaining popularity, a spot on the team, a role in the play, a chair in the band, a niche on the honor roll. The underachievers are doing it by just trying to keep their heads above water.

You know best whether your group tends toward the competitors or the complacent. Keep that assessment in mind as you lead the last four sessions, which deal with four areas in which your students can win or lose. The first is *peer pressure,* a perennial favorite on everyone's must-discuss list; you'll want to emphasize the positive nature of Jesus' example, however, rather than repeating warnings about "going along with the crowd" which your group members have probably learned to ignore. The second is *competition;* tailor your approach according to the makeup of your group, concentrating as needed on either controlling ambition or merely surviving the battle for grades and friends. Third is *self-image,* with an emphasis on the need to let God measure us rather than comparing ourselves to others at school. Fourth is *doubt,* the kind caused by non-Christian teachings and persecution at school; even if most of your students attend Christian schools, you can be sure they've wondered about evolution, situation ethics, and other challenges to their faith.

If you use the sessions, will you ever have to talk with your young people about these subjects again? Yes! Each topic may be worth a quarter's study in itself. These sessions are meant to get your students thinking, to relate the topics and Bible truths specifically to that unique dimension—The School Zone.

WINNING IN THE SCHOOL ZONE

SESSION 9

THE BIG SQUEEZE

KEY CONCEPT

Even Jesus was pressured to do wrong in order to "fit in." He can help us stand up to this temptation at school—and forgive us if we fail to do so.

MEETING THE NEED

This session will respond to student questions and comments like these:

- "Two guys on the basketball team keep asking me when I'm going to grow up and smoke a couple of joints with them. So I ask myself, 'Yeah, when?' "
- "Everybody's always talking about all this 'peer pressure.' What's wrong with not wanting to stick out like a sore thumb?"
- "I'll *die* if I can't get my hair cut that way. All the kids will think I'm a geek if I don't."

SESSION GOALS

You'll help each group member
1. consider the good and bad sides of conformity,
2. see that Jesus was tempted in this area as we are,
3. understand that Jesus forgives us for "giving in" and wants to help us start fresh with Him.

SPECIAL PREPARATION

_____ If you want to try the "Building the Body" activity called "Pop Quiz," bring cola and paper cups as noted in the description of this opening activity.

_____ Contact your "secret agents" for the Pop quiz before the session.

_____ Make copies of the Workout Sheets as usual, but cut Sheet #18 into thirds for the three study groups.

BUILDING THE BODY

To remind your group of the reality of peer pressure, try one or both of the following activities:

"POP" QUIZ

Tell your group that it's time for a "pop" quiz—a taste test like they've seen on TV. Say that you have two different brands of cola (actually the same brand—you've secretly put them in different bottles and covered the labels before the session) and that one is sweeter than the other. You want to find out whether your students' taste buds are smart enough to tell the difference. Have everyone taste "brand" #1 at the same time, then "brand" #2. After the drinks have been tasted, take a person-by-person, row-by-row voice vote on which pop was sweeter. Start with two or more students whom you've contacted before the session and instructed to vote for #2. When all your students have voted, you'll probably find that #2 has been chosen the sweetest. Then reveal that your group has been a victim of peer pressure; you pressed them to believe that the two brands were different, and your "secret agents" further pressed them to believe #2 was sweeter. Use this as an illustration of how we often change our opinions to go along with those around us. (If #1 wins, you can still point out that the group went along with the idea that the brands were different, even if their taste buds told them otherwise.)

WE'VE GOT RHYTHM

Have your group members sit in a circle and close their eyes. Tell them you're going to start a pattern of clapping; they're to match it exactly and keep matching it until the pattern changes. Their eyes must stay closed. From time to time you'll tap a student on the shoulder, which gives him or her permission to change the pattern. The others must immediately adapt to and follow the new pattern until it changes again. After a few minutes of this, call a halt and ask what your students had to do to follow the leader (concentrate and conform). Did those who led prefer leading or following? (Probably leading; you get to make up your own pattern and have a feeling of power.) Point out that we do this sort of thing all the time at school, but with our eyes open. We often look to the trend-setters and copy them—or if we can't, we try not to call too much attention to our being "out of step."

LAUNCHING THE LESSON

WORKOUT SHEET

Distribute Workout Sheet #17, "What's Hot, What's Not." Have students fill in what's "in" and "out" at school, and which trends they'd like to follow. If there are several "hot" styles and activities, depending on one's circle of friends, students should write down the trends they like best. When sheets are completed, regroup and compare answers. If your young teens want to follow a trend, find out why. Do they want to look or act like somebody on TV, in the movies, in a magazine, or just somebody else at school? If nobody else dressed that way or participated in that activity, would they still want to? If they *don't* want to dress or act in the popular style, is it because they think they'd look silly? Because it costs too much? Because parents won't let them? Point out that if we decide either way on the basis of not wanting to look dumb or be left out, it shows that we want to "fit in." Even people who don't always "follow the crowd" don't want to be rejected.

FITTING IN

Say: **It's not wrong to want to fit in. People of all ages want to dress and act more or less like their friends. After all, when was the last time you saw your principal wear a swimsuit to work? He (or she) doesn't want to be laughed at any more than you do. That's why we tend to wear "uniforms"—not *exactly* the same, but not so different that people will think we just arrived from another planet. We tend to talk like our friends too—and act like them. We may like to stand out from our friends in *little* ways, like wearing *slightly* different clothes or getting a better grade on a test—but when it comes to being liked, we like to be alike.**

Sometimes, though, wanting to fit in causes problems. Let's say your friends' favorite way to relax is getting drunk. Tonight your parents are gone and your friends want you to come over to drink. If you don't, maybe you won't fit in with them anymore. What do you do? (Allow students to answer. Whatever solution they propose, point out that they'll end up not "fitting in" with someone—friends, parents, or God—as a result.) **Maybe nobody pressures you to drink. What else might kids at school do that you aren't supposed to do?** (Depending on the sensitivities of your group, these might include dancing, going to some or all movies, looking at a porno magazine or videotape, swearing, smoking, shoplifting, joining a gang, using drugs, cheating, skipping classes, telling dirty jokes, listening to certain music, etc. If some students challenge others about whether all these things are really wrong, defer that debate to another time.) **Maybe you're not pressured by any of those "big" things. How about "little" things, like making fun of the kid in class who has something wrong with him? It's hard not to join in, even if you know God doesn't want you to. And how about things God *wants* you to do, but other kids might think you were weird if you did them?** (These might include witnessing, saying grace before lunch, making friends with a "reject," standing up for the Bible in class, etc.) **It's easier to do the "right" things here in the group where it's "safe." But it's a lot harder out there at school. Nobody there is going to elect you student body president for saying grace or not swearing.**

Do you think anybody ever pressured Jesus to do something wrong or to keep from doing something right? Or was He above all that? (Wait for answers. If you get any, ask for a why or why not.) **As a matter of fact, the Bible says Jesus was tempted in the same ways we are (Hebrews 4:15). Some of the temptations were pretty attractive. Let's find out what they were and what He did about them.**

EXPLORING THE WORD

WORKOUT SHEET

Divide the group into three research teams. Pass out Workout Sheet #18, "Some Offers He Could Refuse" (which you've cut into thirds before the session) to the teams. Have the teams study their verses and answer their Workout Sheet questions. When you get back together, instruct each team to share the results of its research. Use the following comments to further relate Jesus' experiences to the problem of peer pressure:

Team 1—**The Pharisees were pressuring Jesus and His disciples to do things *their* way (Matthew 9:14-15). If the Pharisees had to go without food to show how "holy" they were, then *everybody* had to. They were saying "Look, Jesus, if You don't fast, You can't be a member of the Holy Club. *Everybody* fasts. Why don't You? You must not be as good as we are." Jesus didn't fall for that. He explained that His disciples would fast after He was gone, but for now they felt more like celebrating because He was with them.**

Later Jesus pointed out that no matter what He did, He wouldn't fit in with *somebody* (11:16-19). John the Baptist had sometimes gone without food and drink, so some people said he had a demon. Jesus ate and drank, so some people said He ate too much and was a drunk. What did Jesus mean when He said, "Wisdom is proved right by her actions"? (The wise thing to do turns out right, no matter what people say; you can't depend on the crowd to tell you what's right.)

When Jesus told His disciples He was going to be killed (16:21-23), Peter thought that was the worst idea he'd ever heard. Peter didn't want Jesus to die. But by saying that, he was putting a lot of pressure on Jesus. The Lord didn't look forward to being nailed to a cross. Maybe Peter's words reminded Jesus that if He wanted to, He could get out of being killed. Jesus didn't *have* to obey God and die for our sins. He could have had a comfortable life instead. But Jesus knew the devil was tempting Him through Peter's words; He told Peter, "Out of My sight, Satan!" He said Peter was thinking man's way, not God's.

So when we're pressured at school to fit in by disobeying God, where does that temptation really come from? (The devil.) **If we think Peter's way and worry more about feeling comfortable than about pleasing God, it's going to be *very* hard to stand up to the pressure.**

Team 2—**Satan came right out and tempted Jesus himself this time (Matthew 4:1-11). The devil wanted Jesus to turn stones into bread, but Jesus said no—it was more important to obey God than to have the physical things Jesus wanted (He was *very* hungry after 40 days in the desert). What kinds of physical things might we want in order to fit in or be popular?** (Whatever other kids have—the "right" clothes, electronics, car or bike, a nice house to bring friends to, money to go out with friends, etc.) **It wasn't wrong to eat bread, but it would have been wrong for Jesus *then.* There may be nothing wrong with $50 designer jeans, but God may have other ways for us to spend time and money.**

Then the devil tempted Jesus to do something dangerous—to jump off the temple. Jesus refused. What are some of the dangerous things people might pressure us to do? (Take drugs, steal or otherwise break the law, break a school rule, fight, join a gang, etc.) **Jesus didn't give in to the devil because doing something dangerous for no good reason is like daring God to keep you safe.**

Finally Satan promised to make Jesus powerful and popular—the ruler of the whole world. Jesus would just have to bow down to Satan. Jesus said no, that only God is to be worshiped. This is what the pressure to fit in is all about—wanting to be popular, even to have some power over other kids. If it means obeying the devil instead of God, Jesus said, forget it.

Team 3—**Peter said he'd rather die than deny Jesus (Matthew 26:31-35). But when the pressure was on and Peter knew he might be arrested if he admitted following Jesus, he caved in (26:69-75). He was desperate to fit in, so he said he didn't even *know* Jesus. If some kids at school asked whether you were a Christian, what would you say?** (Allow students to answer.) **Have you ever *not* talked about God at school because it just wouldn't "fit"?** (Wait for an answer. If students are reluctant to admit their failure, you might tell them of a time when you kept quiet about Christ in the face of pressure.) **How do we feel when we let Jesus down that way?** (Probably guilty, sad. Point out that Peter cried bitterly over what he had done.)

Let's face it. We all give in sometimes to this pressure. To fit in, we do things we shouldn't, or don't do things we should. Does God forgive us when we cave in? (Yes. Jesus forgave Peter, as we read in John 21:14-19.) **What did Jesus tell Peter to do in verse 19?** (Follow Him.) **That's what Jesus wants from us now—to follow Him, even at school. If we blow it, He forgives us and helps us to start over. Even if you've been doing wrong things to fit in since you started school, you can ask Him to forgive you today—and start following Him tomorrow. It's up to you. Kids at school may squeeze us to fit into their mold, but God doesn't squeeze. He gives us a choice and wants to help us stand up for Him.**

APPLYING THE TRUTH

STUDENT BOOK OPTION

Ask: **Were Rita and Heather happy being squeezed by peer pressure?** (No, they were in constant fear of making a mistake.) **Did they accept and trust each other?** (No, they "squeezed" each other and probably said nasty things behind each other's backs.) **What does it mean that God doesn't pressure you?** (He wants us to be like Him because we love Him and because it will be good for us—not to fit in or meet someone else's expectations.)

TEMPTATION VIDEO

Split the group again into the three research teams. Each team's assignment: To put on a live "video" (otherwise known as a skit) for the rest of the group. Each "video" should show a student being tempted to compromise in order to fit in at school. The student can refuse to give in to the pressure, or he can give in and suffer the consequences. The teams can use their own ideas, but here are a few to fire their imaginations:

1. Two students pressure a third to help them cheat on a math test.
2. As part of a gang or club initiation, a student is told to lie on the railroad tracks and jump out of the way of the train at the last possible second.
3. In the hallway at school, some students of one race are taunting students of another. One of the students in the first group is pressured to join the name-calling; one in the second group is pressured to fight back.
4. A student is tempted in the desert as Jesus was, but with different rewards (like a new cassette deck, making the honor roll, and being captain of the football team or cheerleading squad) offered in return for disobeying God.

After the "videos" are presented, discuss them and thank the participants. Close by having your young teens talk to God silently about how they've been standing up for Him or giving in to the "big squeeze" put on them by other students. Remind them of the forgiveness and strength God offers.

WINNING IN THE SCHOOL ZONE

SESSION 10

SO YOU WANT TO BE A STAR

KEY CONCEPT

Doing our best in school is good, but we need God's perspective to keep competition from getting out of control.

MEETING THE NEED

This session will respond to student comments like these:

- "You practically *have* to cheat to get a decent grade in that class."
- "The coach wants us to put the team before everything else—*everything.* If I have to miss church, that's just the way it is."
- "If I don't get that part in the play, I may as well give up. It'll mean I'm no good at drama after all."

SESSION GOALS

You'll help each group member

1. identify areas in which he or she wants to excel at school,
2. see the pitfalls of excessive competition,
3. understand that Jesus' idea of being "the best" is to be the servant of all.

SPECIAL PREPARATION

_____ If you plan to play "Cheaters Prosper" (described under "Building the Body"), bring a board game with which most of your students will be familiar.

BUILDING THE BODY

Try one or both of these activities to get your group thinking about competition and its consequences.

THE FAME GAME

Split the group into teams and read the following names aloud one at a time (but not the answers, which are in parentheses). See whether your students can identify these "nostalgia names" according to their reasons for fame. Whichever team gives the most correct answers wins.

1. David Cassidy (pop singer, star of TV's *The Partridge Family*)
2. Mark Spitz (former U.S. Olympic gold-medal-winning swimmer)
3. Thomas Eagleton (U.S. Democratic vice-presidential candidate, 1972, replaced in mid-campaign)
4. Bobby Sherman (pop singer, star of TV's *Here Come the Brides*)
5. Annette Funicello (member of TV's *The Mickey Mouse Club,* star of old beach party movies, more recently seen in peanut butter commercials)
6. Cassius Clay (Muhammad Ali's name when he became a boxer)
7. Judy Carne (woman who regularly said, "Sock it to me" on TV's *Laugh-In*)
8. Mickey Dolenz (member of TV's musical group *The Monkees*)
9. Clifford Irving (author of phony biography of Howard Hughes)

10. SPIRO AGNEW
11. BOB COUSY
12. BOB DENVER
13. DEAN MARTIN
14. SAM ERVIN - NC SENATOR
15. LEW ALCINDOR

You'll probably find that a number of these "oldies" are unfamiliar to many of your young teens. Point out that, as the saying goes, "Fame is fleeting." People are competing every day to stand out in some way, and some make it—only to be forgotten in a few years.

CHEATERS PROSPER X

Bring a board game your students enjoy. Divide the group into teams and play for five minutes or so. Then halt the game long enough to announce that half the players are now required to cheat—to win any way they can. Designate these cheaters and resume the action. The game will likely degenerate into chaos in a couple of minutes or less, at which time you can bring it to an end. Ask the noncheaters how it felt to play against people who didn't follow the rules (frustrating, no fun). Point out that when we try to win in any way we can, we're making other people's lives harder as well as disobeying God.

LAUNCHING THE LESSON

FIRST PLACE

Ask: **Which would you rather be, rich or famous?** (Allow students to answer and give their reasons. Some would probably like to be rich *and* famous.) **Would you rather be first-string quarterback on the football team, or sit on the bench all season?** (Probably first-string quarterback.)

Would you rather win first place in the science fair, or get an honorable mention? (Probably first place.)

Most of us would rather get A's than D's, play first trumpet in the band instead of third chair, or get the leading role in a school play instead of playing the part of a tree trunk in the background. Why is that? (We like to be the best, to be noticed, to feel special, to make our parents proud, etc.) **Some people like to daydream about achieving great success—being elected President of the United States, or maybe just being the best-looking person in the eighth grade. Some would rather do it than dream about it, and they set serious goals.**

WORKOUT SHEET

No matter which kind of person you are, here's your chance to consider what it might take to be a star—maybe not a movie star, but the kind of person who makes it to the top. Distribute Workout Sheet #19, "And the Winner Is. . . ." Have students choose their categories and answer the questions. Allow sufficient time; it may take a few minutes for your young teens to imagine themselves achieving great things. Help them along as needed.

When students finish their sheets, discuss answers as a group. These are all opinion questions, so "right" answers are not necessary. Pay special attention to questions 4 and 5, however, since the temptation to cheat and the definition of success will be important elements of the lesson. Point out that practically every field contains dishonest "shortcuts" that some people will always try—and if you're not sure how to measure success, you may always be trying to reach it and not getting there.

Say: **Even if you don't want to be the *best* at something, you probably don't want to be the worst either. So you get stuck in the competition at school whether you want to or not, competing for grades, places on teams and in bands, parts in plays, awards in contests, and the most votes in class elections. Eventually you may compete for scholarships, jobs, or acceptance at college.**

Whether we want to be stars or just survive, competition can get out of hand and cause us real problems. So we need to know what Jesus said about success and trying to be the best. He may never have tried out for your basketball team, but He's the expert at being the best—because He's perfect.

EXPLORING THE WORD

DISCUSSION PANEL

Form a "discussion panel" of four volunteers and have them sit at the front of the room. Assign each panel member one of the following passages to read aloud. Introduce each reading as noted; then follow up with discussion along the lines suggested. Anyone in the group—not just those on the panel—may participate in the discussion.

Say: **Our first panel member will help us discover whether Jesus thought it was wrong to try to achieve, to make the most of our abilities.** Have panel member #1 read Matthew 25:14-30, the Parable of the Talents. Then explain that a "talent" was a form of money, worth over $1,000. Ask: **What did the master want the servants to do with their talents?** (Invest them so that they ended up with more than they were given.) **What did the good servants do with theirs?** (Put them to work and earned more.) **What did the lazy servant do with his?** (Buried it.) **Who does the master in the story stand for?** (Jesus.) **What did He mean when He said, "Everyone who has will be given more"? (v. 29)** (When we stand before God, He will reward us according to the way we used what He gave us.) **What kinds of "talents" has Jesus entrusted to us to use until He returns?** (Abilities, money, time.) **What does He want us to do with them?** (Make the most of them.) **This story isn't mainly about making money. It's about obeying Jesus while we wait for Him to come back. One way we can serve Him is to use the abilities He's entrusted to us. We have to remember, though, that our talents are "on loan"; they really still belong to God. When we achieve, we're to do it for the Lord, not just for ourselves.**

Panel member #2 will now tell us what Jesus said about some hotshots who thought they were pretty big stars. Have the second panel member read Matthew 23:1-12. Then explain that the phylacteries the teachers wore were little boxes with Scripture verses in them. Ask: **How do we know from this passage that the Pharisees loved to be the "stars"?** (They did everything to be seen by others, or showed off; they made their outfits as impressive as possible; they loved having the best seats at banquets and in the synagogues; they loved to be recognized on the streets and to be called by their titles.) **If people had asked for autographs in those days, the Pharisees would have loved that too. What did Jesus mean in verses 11 and 12?** (Being famous or best or important in people's eyes isn't the same as being great in God's eyes. He says the greatest person is the one who serves others the most. If you blow your own horn and try to be the "star" to draw attention to yourself, God will eventually put you at the end of the line. If you're willing to serve others now, God will eventually make you one of His "stars.") **Most of us would like to be Most Valuable Player or Homecoming Queen or win an Academy Award so that others will look up to us. But Jesus says we should all look up to our Heavenly Father instead.**

Now it's time for panel member #3 to tell us about competition among the disciples. Have that person read Matthew 20:20-28. Explain that the sons of Zebedee were James and John. Ask: **What did the mother of James and John want Jesus to do?** (Make her sons "stars" by giving them the best seats in Jesus' kingdom. She thought Jesus was going to start an earthly kingdom, and hoped He would make her boys the second and third in command.) **How would you feel if you were on the football team and your mother went to the coach and asked, "Coach, won't you let my boy play in the starting lineup this Friday?"** (Probably embarrassed. For some reason James and John weren't.) **Did Jesus agree to do it?** (No. He asked whether they could "drink from His cup"—take the punishment He was going to take—but said only His Father could choose those who would sit at His right and left in heaven.) **What did the other disciples do when they found out what James and John were trying to pull?** (Got mad because *they* wanted a shot at the top spots too.) **What did Jesus tell them about trying to be the greatest?** (If you want to be greatest, you have to be everyone's servant.) **What did He say the Gen-**

tiles did instead? (They liked to "lord it over" each other.) **Jesus could have lorded it over us because He *is* the Lord. But He served all of us by dying for us. When we try to push each other out of the way to get to the top, we're not following Jesus' example.**

Panel member #4 will tell us what the Apostle Paul wrote about Jesus and competition. Have this panel member read Philippians 2:3-11. Then ask: **What three rules about competition does Paul give us in verses 3 and 4?** (Don't do things out of selfish ambition or conceit; consider others better than yourself; and care about others' interests as well as your own.) **What's selfish ambition?** (Trying to reach your goal for your own glory, even at the expense of others.) **What's vain conceit?** (Thinking you're more important than you really are.) **What does Paul mean by "consider others better than yourselves"?** (He doesn't mean we should think we're uglier or more sinful than others; he means we shouldn't insist on being first. We should have the attitude of a servant who knows his "place" is to help others.) **Let's say you're competing in a speech tournament. How could you look out for others' interests as well as your own?** (Be friendly and thoughtful to other contestants; don't try to distract them or put them down; don't cheat; don't rub it in if they lose, etc.) **If we follow these three rules of competition, can we cheat on a test or on our homework?** (No. First of all, cheating is lying—turning in work that isn't really yours—and it's stealing if you've copied someone else's answers. It's also a form of selfish ambition because it ignores the effect cheating has on those who *don't* cheat; if a teacher grades on a curve, a cheater may be causing honest students to get lower grades. You can't look out for others' interests and steal their answers or be unfair to them by cheating.) **Paul says we should be like Jesus, the greatest servant. Jesus practiced what He preached about being a servant instead of a star. What has God done for Jesus as a result of His being such a servant?** (Exalted Him to the highest place—made Him the greatest star, One who will never fade.) **God will also reward *us* in heaven if we've been servants instead of selfish stars. That means all of us can "be somebody" someday—even if we don't get the trophies and blue ribbons now. We can do our best with the abilities God has loaned us, using them to serve others instead of ourselves.**

APPLYING THE TRUTH

STUDENT BOOK OPTION

Read the example of Sheila, whose speech team adviser wanted everyone to make speech the top priority. Ask: **What issues does this bring up for a Christian like Sheila?** (A highly competitive spirit may lead the team to despise or look down on competitors. There's nothing wrong with winning, but bad or selfish motives are wrong. Stewardship of time is also an issue. How much time should be devoted to a single activity that takes time away from other important things?)

WORKOUT SHEET

Distribute Workout Sheet #20, "Crossing the Line." Have your students fill out their sheets, showing which ways of competing go too far. Then regroup to share answers. These are opinion questions, so try not to come down too hard on those with whom you disagree. Instead, ask them to explain how their answers fit with the biblical principles you've discussed. Then conclude by making the following points about school competition and Christians:

1. ***Doing your best is more important than winning or being a star.*** **"Whatever your hand finds to do, do it with all your might" (Ecclesiastes 9:10). The Bible doesn't say anything about having to win or be famous.**

2. ***Do your best to bring glory to God, who loaned you your talent—not just for your satisfaction or to get others to look up to you.*** **"Whatever you do, work at it with all your heart, as working for the Lord, not for men" (Colossians 3:23).**

3. ***If you do an outstanding job, don't forget to thank God and give Him credit.*** **Eric Liddell, a Christian who won a medal as a runner in the 1924 Olympics, told people that when he ran he could feel God's pleasure. Now millions of people know who gave Eric his talent, having heard Eric's words in the movie *Chariots of Fire*.**

4. ***Don't let fear of failing push you to cheat, or try so hard that you burn out, or give up if you don't reach your goal.*** **God has promised to meet all your needs; you don't have to be "the best" to survive. "My God will meet all your needs according to His glorious riches in Christ Jesus" (Philippians 4:19). Stars may worry about reaching and staying at the top—but servants don't have to worry about a thing.**

WINNING IN T SCHOOL ZON

SESSION 11

WHEN YOU DON'T MEASURE UP

KEY CONCEPT

Comparing ourselves with others at school can make us feel like failures; remembering how God sees us can help us feel worthwhile.

MEETING THE NEED

This session will respond to student comments like these:

- "I hate P.E. class because we have to change clothes, and I still look like a little kid compared with the others."
- "The other kids seem to catch on right away in Spanish class. I'd rather die than try to pronounce the words because I always get them wrong."
- "I keep thinking the other kids are staring at me because I'm so ugly and trip over everything."

SESSION GOALS

You'll help each group member

1. identify areas in which he is unfavorably comparing himself with others at school,
2. see that worth comes from God, not from oneself or from others,
3. consider the positive, unique qualities God has given him or her.

SPECIAL PREPARATION

_____ Using the "Building the Body" activity called "What's It Worth?" will require a variety of household items and a list of their prices which you've checked at the store.

_____ If you plan to use the "Everybody's Olympics" opener, bring the paper clips, pencils, and marbles needed for the contests—as well as prizes for the winners.

_____ Bring a tape recorder and microphone to record the "mental tapes" as described under "Launching the Lesson" and "Applying the Truth."

BUILDING THE BODY

Use one of the following activities to get your students thinking about their own value.

WHAT'S IT WORTH?

Play your own version of the TV game show, *The Price Is Right.* Collect six or seven household items (food, cleaning supplies, etc.) and check their prices at a local supermarket. Bring the items and your price list to the meeting; divide the group into teams whose job is to guess the items' prices. Be sure to tell the players which store's prices are being used as the standard, to avoid arguments later. The winning team is the one whose total "grocery bill" of guesses comes closest to the actual total. Point out later that just as the guesses were often under or over the actual prices, we find it hard to measure how much *we* are worth. And just as a manufacturer sets the "manufacturer's suggested retail price" of an item, God knows best how much we are worth—because He created us.

EVERYBODY'S OLYMPICS

Your young teens are used to entering (and often losing) school competitions which measure mental, artistic, or athletic skills. Give them a chance to win by demonstrating *other* traits or abilities. Emphasize fun rather than competition as you determine who can:

1. Unbend a paper clip and make it straightest in a total of three seconds;
2. Name the most fruits or vegetables that start with the same letter as his own last name;
3. Do the best impression of a person, machine, or musical instrument;
4. Find the Book of Philemon fastest;
5. Tell the shortest joke;
6. Balance the most pencils on his head;
7. Roll a marble the slowest (without it stopping) across the floor;
8. Produce the oldest wallet or heaviest purse.

If time allows, add other events that will allow as many group members as possible to win prizes. Then explain that school contests don't measure most of the things that are special about us. And *no* contest, whether it's running hurdles or rolling marbles, can label a person a "failure."

LAUNCHING THE LESSON

WORKOUT SHEET

Distribute Workout Sheet #21, "The Big, Small Measurement Test." Have your students match the kinds of measurements with their units of measure. Answers are as follows: 1-M; 2-H; 3-G; 4-K; 5-O; 6-N; 7-C; 8-D; 9-E; 10-B; 11-I; 12-F; 13-J; 14-A; 15-L. After revealing the answers and congratulating the person with the highest score, say: **The world is full of measurements. We're always measuring things to find out who sets a record,**

who has the most money, who has the biggest house. We just used a measure—the number of right answers—to figure out who did well on the measurement test. But if you don't use the right kind of measurement, you won't get the right answer. If you try to measure your height in ounces or miles per hour, you won't be able to find out how tall you are.

MEASURING UP

It's the same way at school. We're always measuring things there. What are some of the ways your teachers measure your performance? (Grades, tests, how much you participate in class, how smart you sound, how many push-ups you can do, etc.) **How do other kids measure how worthwhile you are?** (The way you look; the clique you're in; how much money your family has; where you live; whether you're athletic, artistic, or otherwise talented; the way you talk; who your friends are, etc.) **And how do you measure for yourself how worthwhile you are?** (By comparing yourself to others, to what others say about you, to people on TV and in magazines, and sometimes to what the Bible says.)

STUDENT BOOK OPTION

Ask: **Does Roger's learning disability make him a failure?** (Though some people may think so, stress that failing at something doesn't make a *person* a failure. Roger has worth as a human being.) **How does God view Roger?** (He cares about his problem, but He is more interested in Roger's relationship to Jesus.)

TAPE RECORDER

All this measurement can cause problems. If teachers and students compare you to other people, and if you compare yourself to others, you're always going to be taller or shorter or faster or slower or have stringier hair than somebody else. Let's say you're in P.E. class, and you're having a hard time getting through all those jumping jacks. Suddenly the teacher sees that you weigh a little more than somebody else, so he yells at you, "You're so fat that when you step on a scale, the springs pop out!" At this point bring out the tape recorder you've brought and ask one of your students to repeat the "fat" insult into the microphone, recording it. Do the same thing with different students after each of the following put-downs, getting them on tape one after another. **Or you give a wrong answer in class, and the kid next to you says, "You're so stupid that if you took out your brain, you'd be smarter!"** (Have a student repeat as you record.) **Or another kid says, "Your nose is so big that if it were green, people would mistake it for a cucumber!"** (Repeat, record.) **Or another kid says, "You're so ugly that if you went to the zoo, they wouldn't let you out!"** (Repeat, record.) **Or you miss a shot on the basketball court and the coach says,"You're so clumsy you could cut yourself on a balloon!"** (Repeat, record.) **Or still another kid says, "Your breath is so bad that if you whistled in a graveyard, the tombstones would curl up and die!"** (Repeat, record.)

Rewind the tape as you say: **Now, if you keep hearing things like that, or if you keep comparing yourself to others at school who are skinnier or get better grades or have smaller noses or are more popular, you're going to hear this kind of thing over and over in your mind.** Play the tape of put-downs you've just recorded. Then explain: **You can end up putting yourself down again and again if you compare yourself to others or let others decide what you're worth. Sooner or later you can feel like a total failure. But it doesn't have to be that way. Before you decide that you don't measure up at school, you need to make sure who's got the right measuring stick. That's what we're going to find out in the Bible today.**

EXPLORING THE WORD

TEAM INVESTIGATION

Divide the group into three investigative teams. Team A will find out how Jesus could have felt inferior by comparing Himself with others or accepting their measurement of Him; Team B will discover how Jesus treated people who didn't "measure up"; and Team C will see how God's standards differ from ours. Assign Team A to read John 1:45-46; Matthew 8:20; 9:23-24, 32-34; and 27:15-26. Team B should read Matthew 3:1-4, 11-15; 11:7-12, 18; Luke 19:1-10; and Mark 1:40-42. Team C should read Matthew 6:25-27; Romans 3:22-24; 1 Samuel 16:6-7; and Micah 6:8. When the teams are finished, bring them back together.

Ask Team A: **According to the verses you read, what reasons might Jesus have had for feeling inferior to other people?** (He came from the "wrong" place, Nazareth, a town which didn't get much respect [John 1:45-46]; He was poor—so poor He didn't have a place to live [Matthew 8:20]; people didn't understand Him and laughed at Him [Matthew 9:23-24]; others said He was demon-possessed, which was about the worst thing you could be [Matthew 9:32-34]; and when people had a chance to choose between Him and a criminal, they chose the criminal and said Jesus deserved to die [Matthew 27:15-26]). **What do your verses say about the way Jesus looked? Was He handsome or not so good-looking?** (The Bible doesn't say.) **Well, why doesn't the Bible tell us? Don't we need to know?** (No; it's not important.) **Sometimes we think the way we look is the most important thing in the world—that everybody is staring at our pimples or the way we just couldn't get our hair to do the right thing this morning. But none of the Bible writers ever bothered to write a word about Jesus' looks—because it wasn't important.**

Looking back, we may think Jesus had no reason to feel bad about Himself. But if He'd just compared Himself with others, or believed their put-downs, He could have felt like a failure. Why do you suppose He didn't? (Because He's the Son of God and knows that He's perfect.) **A son of God would have no reason to feel like a failure. So look up John 1:12 and find out who you are if you've received Jesus as your Saviour.** (Children of God, sons of God.) **We're not perfect as Jesus was, but we're sons and daughters of God. How does God feel about His sons and daughters?** (Loves them.) **If we accept His Son Jesus, then God accepts us. Jesus knew it wasn't important to compare Himself with others to measure up; He was already accept-**

ed and loved by His Heavenly Father, and so are we.

Then ask Team B: **In your verses, whom did Jesus talk with?** (John the Baptist, Zaccheus, and a leper.) **What reasons did those people have to feel "not good enough"?** (John the Baptist ate strange food, wore strange clothes, said he wasn't fit to untie Jesus' sandals, and people said he had a demon; Zaccheus was short and people said he was a sinner because he was a crooked tax collector; disease made the leper an outcast, repulsive to others because of the way leprosy deforms a person and because people feared catching it.) **How did Jesus treat these three people?** (He asked John to baptize Him [Matthew 3:13-14] and said there had never been a greater person than John [11:11]; Jesus talked with Zaccheus, stayed at his house, and said Zaccheus would be saved [Luke 19:5-10]; in addition to talking with the leper, Jesus did something no one else would do—He touched the man and healed him [Mark 1:40-42].) **Others thought these three were weird or worthless. In some ways the three of them probably *felt* worthless. Did Jesus measure them by the same standards?** (No. He saw the faith they had, instead of looking at their appearances, reputations, or even their feelings about themselves.)

Then ask Team C: **Read Matthew 6:25-27. What did Jesus say about worrying over our appearance?** (He said not to worry about our bodies or our clothes because God would take care of us—and worrying wouldn't do any good anyway.) **Did He say we were worth anything to Him?** (We're much more valuable than the sparrows, and God takes care of them.) **In Romans 3:22-24, what does it say about the standard God uses to measure us?** (We have all fallen short of His glory, His perfection.) **Do good-looking people or kids who get straight A's meet His standard?** (No. Nobody does.) **If we don't meet His standard, does God reject us?** (Not if we put our faith in Jesus.) **What did God tell Samuel (1 Samuel 16:6-7) about how He measures a person?** (He doesn't consider appearance or height, but looks at the heart—the real person inside.) **According to Micah 6:8, what does God require of a person?** (To act justly, love mercy, and walk humbly with Him.) **Isn't there something there about having to talk without stuttering, or being able to color-coordinate your clothes, or having perfect teeth?** (Nope.)

God doesn't figure out how much we're worth by comparing us with other people. He has His own perfect standards, and they have nothing to do with the measuring sticks used by most people at school. And unlike some people at school, God doesn't just hold us up to His ruler and say, "Sorry, you flunk," and throw us away. He gives us a chance to put our faith in Jesus—who didn't judge by other people's standards either—so that we can become His sons and daughters, loved and accepted by Him.

APPLYING THE TRUTH

WORKOUT SHEET

Distribute Workout Sheet #22, "Put-ups." Allow plenty of time for your young teens to think of positive things about themselves; many of them aren't used to it. If needed, help by suggesting some of the following:

1. "I've got (nice ankles, all my fingers, lots of freckles)."

2. "I can (thread a needle, play the guitar, be a good listener)."
3. "God (loves me, accepts me, wants me to come and live with Him someday)."
4. "I feel (glad that God loves me, safe with Him protecting me, like I want to serve Him)."
5. "God will (take me to heaven, answer my prayers, never leave me)."

When your students have completed their sheets, bring out your tape recorder again and record some of their positive statements. As you rewind the tape, ask a student to read Philippians 4:8 aloud. Then summarize: **God wants us to think about things that are true, noble, right, pure, lovely, admirable, excellent, and praiseworthy. Instead of putting ourselves down and believing others who put us down, we can run this kind of "tape" in our minds.** Play the tape of positive statements. Then conclude with prayer, thanking God for the worth He has given each of your students—a value that no one can take away.

WINNING IN THE SCHOOL ZONE

SESSION 12

FOR DOUBTERS ONLY

KEY CONCEPT

Non-Christian teachings and persecution at school can cause us to doubt our beliefs, but dealing honestly with our doubts can end up strengthening our faith.

MEETING THE NEED

This session will respond to student questions and comments like these:

- "My science teacher says the Bible is full of myths. Sometimes I think he's right. Is God mad at me for doubting?"
- "Some kids at school think 'religious' people are nerds. I'm afraid to say anything 'Christian' around them."
- "Is it dumb to be a Christian?"

SESSION GOALS

You'll help each group member

1. realize that those who knock the Bible and Christianity are no threat to God, and their comments are to be expected,
2. see that God does not reject us for sometimes doubting Him,
3. consider reasons for keeping the faith despite criticism from others at school.

SPECIAL PREPARATION

_____ Draw the three "doodles" on a chalkboard or flip chart if you plan to use the "Building the Body" activity called "What Is It?"

_____ Make copies of the skit, "How Do You Spell BELIEF?" (found under "Launching the Lesson") and practice with cast members before the session.

_____ If you'd like to provide your students with extra resources on the reasonableness of Christianity, bring a few copies of *Know What You Believe* and *Know Why You Believe* by Paul Little (Victor Books) to loan them.

BUILDING THE BODY

Try one or both of these activities to get your young teens thinking about what happens when they aren't given all the facts.

HALF-TRUTH

One at a time, have each group member make two statements about himself; one is to be true, the other a lie. The truths should sound unlikely and the lies believable, in order to fool the rest of the group. After each person makes his or her statements, have the group vote on which statement is true. Whoever fools the most people wins. Besides helping your students get to know each other a little better, this activity enables you to point out that truth can sound too crazy to believe—and lies can seem to make a lot of sense. Later in the lesson, use this as an analogy to the mixture of truths and falsehoods we hear at school.

WHAT IS IT?

Draw the following "doodles" on a chalkboard or flip chart:

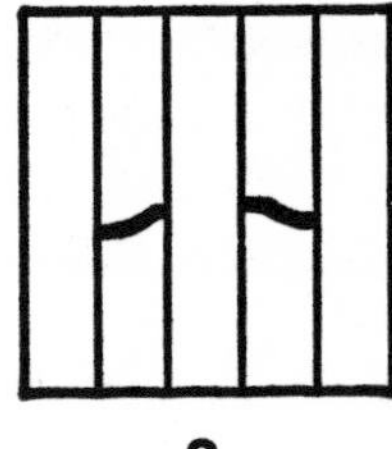

1 2 3

Challenge your students to figure out what the drawings represent. You'll get a variety of answers, but the *right* ones are these: (1) A three-year-old's birthday cake, viewed from above; (2) What Zorro wrote on the wall before he fell in the water; and (3) A snake seen through prison bars. Explain that we can come to the wrong conclusions if we decide without having "the whole picture." Later, relate this to the fact that many people have decided to reject Christianity without knowing much about it. And many have accepted theories like evolution even though the "evidence" is far from complete.

LAUNCHING THE LESSON

SKIT

Begin by having four of your students perform the following skit, "How Do You Spell BELIEF?" Make enough copies before the session so that each cast member has one; practice the play during the week and/or before the rest of the group arrives. This version of the familiar Rolaids commercial includes a microphone-holding reporter and three people on the street. Remind your actors to say the word "belief" carefully so that no one mistakes it for "relief," and to spell out the words which have hyphens between the letters.

REPORTER: This is your man-on-the-street reporter for Schoola-Seltzer, the antacid that helps you through those tough times at school—those times when you feel like doubting your faith. (*Enter Girl #1.*) Ah, here's someone we can talk to. Excuse me, Miss.
GIRL #1: Yes?
REPORTER: Miss, I'm taking a survey for Schoola-Seltzer. We'd like to know: How do you spell BELIEF?
GIRL #1: *(suddenly scared)* B-b-belief? I spell it F-E-A-R!
REPORTER: F-E-A-R? Why, that spells "fear"!
GIRL #1: I—I know. Sometimes when I'm in science class and the teacher starts talking about evolution, I wonder whether he's right and the Bible is wrong. (*She looks around as if expecting to be struck by lightning.*) Oh, I'm sure God must be so mad at me! He must hate it when I d-d-d—
REPORTER: Doubt?
GIRL #1: Oh, don't say that word! I just know He's going to punish me for questioning! I'd better get out of here before I get hit by lightning or a tornado. . . . (*She runs out.*)
REPORTER: Uh, thank you. (*Enter Guy.*) Ah, here's someone else we can survey. Pardon me, Sir. How do you spell BELIEF?
GUY: (*robotlike, as if repeating what he's been taught*) I spell it M-O-M-A-N-D-D-A-D.
REPORTER: Let's see. . . . That spells . . . "Mom and Dad."
GUY: Correct.
REPORTER: Well, what do Mom and Dad have to do with belief?
GUY: I believe whatever they believe.
REPORTER: I see. And what do they believe?
GUY: I don't know.
REPORTER: Then how do you know whether you believe it?
GUY: I just do. I do not wish to think about it. It is too hard. I would rather go along with whatever they say and the church says, even if I don't know what it is.
REPORTER: Well, do you ever doubt your faith?
GUY: Faith? What is faith? That does not compute. (*He exits.*)
REPORTER: Hmm. How can you believe without faith? (*Enter Girl #2.*) Well, let's try one more. Excuse me, Miss. How do you spell BELIEF?
GIRL #2: (*casually*) Belief? I'd rather not spell it at all. But if I did, it would be L-A-T-E-R.
REPORTER: But that spells "later."
GIRL #2: I know. I'd rather not worry about that stuff now. I'll just leave it up in the air and not come down on one side or the other. Maybe Christianity's true, maybe it isn't. Maybe I can trust the Bible, maybe not.
REPORTER: But when are you going to start thinking about these things and making up your mind?
GIRL #2: Oh, I don't know. Later. Maybe when I'm real old, like 30 or 40.
REPORTER: But what if you don't live that long? And how are you going to live if you don't know what you believe?
GIRL #2: (*shrugging*) I don't know. I'll have to think about that one—later. See you . . . later! (*She exits.*)
REPORTER: (*with a sigh*) I give up. Looks like nobody knows how to spell BELIEF. This is your man on the street for Schoola-Seltzer, reminding you that when you learn how to spell BELIEF, it's a real RELIEF. (*He exits.*)

DISCUSSION

After the skit, applaud the participants and discuss the topic of belief and doubt along the following lines: **Does anything you hear at school ever disagree with what you hear at church?** (Wait for responses. Possible answers might include teachings about evolution; the view that all religions are alike or that the Bible is a collection of fables; challenging questions or taunts from other students; sex education without moral content, etc. If you are using the student book, review the things Bruce faced at school that caused him to doubt the truth of Christianity.) **These things sometimes cause us to doubt God or the Bible. How did the people in the play deal with their doubts?** (They didn't; one was too scared, one didn't want to think for himself, and one wanted to wait indefinitely.) **Have you ever had any doubts, even little ones? What did you do about them?** (Allow students to respond.) **The Bible has some things to say about doubt, as well as the things people say that cause us to doubt. Let's use it to find out how to spell "belief."**

EXPLORING THE WORD

WORKOUT SHEET

Distribute Workout Sheet #23, "Just the Facts, Ma'am." After students fill it out, have volunteers read their articles. Use the following summaries as needed:

John 20:24-29 (The doubting disciple was Thomas, who wouldn't believe Jesus had risen from the dead unless he could see the Lord and touch His wounds. Later Jesus appeared to Thomas, but He didn't get angry over the man's doubt. He told Thomas to touch His hands and side to prove to himself that Jesus really was alive. This incident shows us that we don't need to fear that God will reject us for doubting; He wants us to draw close to Him and His Word, to discover that the Bible is true and Jesus is worth following. At the end of this passage, Jesus blesses those who believe in Him *without* seeing Him. He's talking about us; He knew it would be harder to believe now. Instead of getting mad at us, He understands.)

Matthew 5:10-12 (Jesus obviously expected that His followers would be insulted, persecuted, and lied about. And they have been throughout history; many have been thrown in prison or killed for being Christians. Persecution in our schools is far less severe, but it still hurts to be made fun of for believing "that stuff." Jesus promised that He would reward us for sticking with Him. He also said that when we are persecuted for His sake we are like the prophets, who were rejected because they spoke God's messages. This reminds us that when people reject us for being Christians, they are rejecting God; we may hurt, but we don't need to take it personally.)

Hebrews 11:1-3; Matthew 17:18-21 (Faith is being sure of what we hope for but can't see. God knows perfectly well that we can't see Him, yet He wants us to believe anyway. The writer of Hebrews specifically mentions the fact that it takes faith to believe that God created the universe, since none of us were around at the time. How much faith does it take? Jesus said that only a tiny bit, the size of a mustard seed, would move a mountain if God and we agreed that it should move. We don't need more than that to believe in God enough to get close to Him, to ask Him to help us with our doubts, and teach us about Him and His Word.)

So how do you spell "belief"? F-A-I-T-H. Faith doesn't mean you accept something you *know* isn't true; it doesn't mean you turn your brain off and say you believe whatever your parents or teachers believe; it doesn't mean being afraid to doubt. Faith is trusting God to explain the things you don't understand yet. You won't learn all the answers overnight, and you don't have to make up your mind about everything right away. But God wants you to get started now, not "later" when you're old—so that He can make your years in school some of the best of your life.

APPLYING THE TRUTH

WORKOUT SHEET

Distribute Workout Sheet #24, "The Great Debate." Have your students look up and paraphrase the verses that "answer" the questions on the sheet. When they're done, split the group into two debating teams. The question to be debated: "Is It Dumb to Be a Christian?" Give both teams a couple of minutes to review their Workout Sheets and plan strategy. After the debate begins, avoid a free-for-all by starting with the "yes" side and having the "no" side respond. Issues should be limited to those raised on the Workout Sheet unless you have extra time. Help the "no" side along as needed by pointing out the following (numbered to correspond with the Workout Sheet):

1. Evolution *doesn't* show that God didn't create the world. The theory of evolution is changing all the time, trying to explain why there's so little fossil evidence to back it up. As Job was reminded (Job 38:1-7), God was the only One around when the world was made; our theories are only guesses. Science is never complete because it's always learning new things, but God knew the whole story when He inspired the Bible. When it comes to science and the Bible agreeing, it's just a matter of time and learning to interpret the information we have. When you look at all the things in the Bible which can easily be proven true (prophecies that were fulfilled, historical facts confirmed by archeology, etc.), it's almost harder *not* to believe in God's Word than it is to accept it.

2. Of *course* you can't see God. That's no surprise to Him. But as the Apostle Paul wrote (Romans 1:18-20), people have no excuse for not believing in God. That's because His whole creation is all around them, showing that *someone* must have designed it. How could such a beautiful and complex place be an accident?

3. Some Christians are boring, but that's not the Lord's fault. Some non-Christians are boring too! Jesus wants us to "have life, and have it to the full" (John 10:10). When people say Christianity is dull, they usually mean they think Christians aren't supposed to do all the "fun" things some non-Christians do—like getting drunk and smoking. Are car wrecks and lung cancer really that much fun? Jesus wants to replace cheap thrills with the

adventure of living close to the One who created us and has great plans for our futures.

4. Jesus said that He is the only way to reach God (John 14:6). That's not our personal opinion; it's what Jesus Himself said. All we can do is repeat it; people who disagree have a bone to pick with Jesus, not with us. We shouldn't make fun of people who believe in other religions, but we can't throw out Jesus' claim either. He is the only spiritual leader who claimed to be God and then rose from the dead to prove it.

5. Some Christians *are* weak, weird, and crazy. But it's not because they're Christians. God didn't give Jesus' followers a spirit of timidity (wimpiness), but of power, love, and self-discipline (2 Timothy 1:7-8). Jesus calls His followers to action, even to suffer for Him. How many people would be willing to suffer and die for their belief that Christianity *isn't* true? And many things seem weird and crazy until you understand them—like foreign languages, math, and the rules of most sports. Are those who reject Christianity open-minded enough to really try to understand it?

Wind down your "Great Debate" after these points are covered or when time is running out. Note any unresolved questions that have surfaced during the session, and agree to discuss them in the near future. If possible, have a few copies of *Know What You Believe* and *Know Why You Believe* by Paul Little (Victor Books) available to loan interested students. These books will give your young teens more detailed answers to questions raised during the debate.

Don't worry if you haven't been able to deal with all group members' doubts in this session. The most important truth you can leave with them is that God understands our questions and wants to teach us the answers in His way and time. That's the beginning of real, personal faith—the kind that can stand up to any challenge in The School Zone.

JUST THE FACTS, MA'AM

WORKOUT SHEET **23**

Starting with the headlines and verses below, write three short "newspaper" articles. In the first, tell who doubted, how, and why, and how Jesus responded. In the second, tell what Jesus said about being persecuted for following Him. In the third, tell what faith is, how much is necessary, and what it can do.

Holy Land Herald

DOUBTING DISCIPLE DUMBFOUNDED

(John 20:24-29)

TEACHER TELLS TOUGH TIMES

(Matthew 5:10-12)

FANTASTIC FRUIT FLOWS FROM FINITE FAITH

(Hebrews 11:1-3; Matthew 17:18-21)

THE GREAT DEBATE

WORKOUT SHEET 24

IS IT DUMB TO BE A CHRISTIAN?

Look up the verses on the right and summarize them in the blanks before you begin your debate.

YES ⟷ NO

"It's dumb to believe in the Bible when evolution shows that God didn't create the world."	Job 38:1-7	______________________ ______________________
"It's dumb to believe in God; after all, you can't see Him."	Romans 1:18-20	______________________ ______________________
"It's dumb to be a Christian because following Jesus is boring."	John 10:10	______________________ ______________________
"It's dumb to be a Christian because any religion will get you to heaven."	John 14:6	______________________ ______________________
"It's dumb to be a Christian; Christians are all weak, weird, or crazy."	2 Timothy 1:7-8	______________________ ______________________

THE SCHOOL ZONE
EVALUATION SHEET

Dear Leader,
You can have a real impact on future Young Teen Feedback Electives! Please take a minute to fill out this form giving us your candid reaction to this material. Thanks for your help.

ABOUT YOU
In what setting did you use this elective? (Sunday School, youth group, midweek Bible study, etc.) ______

How many young people were in your group? ______

What was the age-range of those in your group? ______

How many weeks did you spend on this study? ______

How long was your average meeting time? ______

(Optional) Name ______

Address ______

ABOUT THIS YOUNG TEEN FEEDBACK ELECTIVE
Did you and your young people enjoy this study? (Why or why not?)

What are the strengths and weaknesses of this leader's book?

Did you use the student books? ______ Yes ______ No
If so, what are their strengths and weaknesses?

ABOUT THE FUTURE
What topics and issues would you like to see covered in future electives?

What Bible studies would you like to see included in future electives?

Do you plan to use other Young Teen Feedback Electives? (Why or why not?)

Do you plan to repeat this study in the future with new students? (Why or why not?)

Place
stamp
here

SonPower Youth Sources Editor
1825 College Avenue
Wheaton, Illinois 60187